KU-287-892

the

Scots

Travelmate

LEXUS

Published 2005 by Lexus Ltd
60 Brook Street, Glasgow G40 2AB
Reprinted 2006

Maps drawn by András Bereznay
Typeset by Elfreda Crehan
Illustrations by Elfreda Crehan

Contributors

Catherine Brown, *food writer*
Sophie Cadell
Fiona Jardine
Domhnall Uilleam Stiùbhart
Birgit Wagner

Series editor: Peter Terrell

© Lexus Ltd

All rights reserved. No part of this publication may reproduced or stored in any form without permission from Lexus Ltd, except for the use of short sections in reviews.

www.lexusforlanguages.co.uk

British Library Cataloguing in Publication Data
A catalogue record for this book is available from the British Library.

ISBN-10: 1-904737-07-2
ISBN-13: 978-1-904737-07-0

Printed and bound in Great Britain by Scotprint

Let's say there are three Scotlands. The Scotland of cities, stunning and gaunt. The Scotland of open spaces, stunning and grand. The Scotland of the mind: inventors of television and telephone, proponents of the existence of underwater monsters, a world of jigs and reels and long traditions, a nation which was independent in heart and mind and stance long before it had its own new parliament.

This book is a guide to the distinct Scots language, urban, rural and cultural. It is aimed both at native speakers of English and those who have learned English as a second language. It explains and exemplifies Scots vocabulary and usage and, on occasions, makes comparisons with English usage, particularly where the differences are likely to cause confusion.

These are assorted fragments of language; you're not going to find any one person in Scotland who uses all these words. The language is often remarkably localized. Scottish people from certain parts of the country or certain walks of life may well not understand some of these words (which does not decrease their Scottishness).

A few of the words listed are showing their age and are now less used in speech. These are marked OLDER SCOTS. By contrast, new words spring up. A good number of these have been labelled SLANG. And the slang is often quite regional, GLASGOW, west coast,

Edinburgh, EAST COAST, Aberdonian or NORTH EAST. At the peripheries, words may spill over into northern English usage. And others (**manky**, **mingin**) which not long ago would doubtless have been only Scottish are now general English usage too. The levelling and homogenizing effects of the mass media and employment mobility, dampers on regional uniqueness, also provide carriers for catchy language to spread across borders. But, in spite of this, Scots retains its own distinct body of language.

Different spellings of Scots words are shown as well as standardized Scots spellings of English words (like heid or deid).

There are explanations of key place name elements, words which, like linguistic time capsules, remind us of the lives of the inhabitants of this country many centuries ago.

Alphabetically merged with the vocabulary are notes on key words from Scottish history and notes on cultural traditions and festivals.

You'll also find:

- an introduction to Scottish food and drink on pages 141–153
- a tiny smattering of Gaelic on pages 154–155
- some place names that are not pronounced as you might think on page 156
- maps of Scotland on pages 157–160.

A

a' all; everything

aa NORTH EAST all; everything

aabody NORTH EAST everybody

aald SHETLAND old

aaricht, aaright NORTH EAST all right

aathing NORTH EAST everything

abeen NORTH EAST OLDER SCOTS above

aber IN PLACE NAMES This **Brittonic** word means *mouth.* So **Aberdeen**: Donsmouth; **Lochaber**: the mouth of the loch.

ablow OLDER SCOTS below

abuin, abune OLDER SCOTS above

ach IN PLACE NAMES from the Gaelic ***achadh*** meaning *field.* So **Achnasheen**: storm field.

adee → NORTH EAST **fit's adee?** what's wrong?

advocate LEGAL SCOTS An **advocate** is a member of the Faculty of Advocates, the governing body of the Scottish legal system. They are often called on to give expert opinions. In Aberdeen, however, the word advocate just means a *lawyer.*

advocate depute LEGAL SCOTS a law officer appointed by the **Lord Advocate** to assist in the administration of mainly criminal matters

ae NORTH EAST one
there's ae thing for sure one thing's for sure

aenoo NORTH EAST just now, right now

aff off

affa NORTH EAST awfully
he's affa nae weel he's not very well
it's affa cold in here it's really cold in here

> **Affa** in Scots is not posh like the English cognate *awfully.*

affie afternoon
aw affie all afternoon

affy very; awfully (but not posh in Scots)

afore OLDER SCOTS before

after → **and that was me just after ma tea** and I had just had my supper
I was just after having a wee drink I had just had a drink

see you after confusing to the non-Scots speaker; after what?, they'll think; but this just means *see you later, cheerio*

ages with To be **ages with someone** means to be the same age as that person.
jings!, I didna realize you were

ages with Uncle Jack!

agley OLDER SCOTS awry, wrong; crooked
the best laid plans of mice and men gang aft agley a much-quoted line from Robert Burns. Often just the first part is said: **ach well, the best laid plans...**

ah rendering of the first person pronoun *I*

ahin(t) NORTH EAST behind

aiblins OLDER SCOTS perhaps

ain own

aince OLDER SCOTS once

aipple apple

airchie NORTH EAST posh, high-class

airt 1) OLDER SCOTS direction; region 2) art
back tae his hame airt back to his own part of the world
in rural airts in rural areas

ald NORTH EAST old

ale NORTH EAST In the North East **ale** is any fizzy drink (like **ginger** in Glasgow). It isn't beer.

alow NORTH EAST below

amna OLDER SCOTS am not; aren't (when used with *I*)

anaith NORTH EAST beneath

anent OLDER SCOTS about, concerning

aneth NORTH EAST under

angina-on-a-plate a humorous name

for a Scottish invention, the deep-fried Mars® Bar, which you can buy at (some) fish and chip shops

Antonine Wall This is the 37 mile long Roman wall which spanned Scotland at its narrowest point from the Firth of Forth to the Firth of Clyde. It was constructed around 139 AD on the orders of the Roman Emperor Antoninus Pius. The wall was built of turf with a broad ditch to the north. Its purpose was to defend the northern boundary of the Roman Empire. But it was only occupied for a short time. Several forts and signal towers have been uncovered and the most visible remains of the wall can be seen near Falkirk.

ard IN PLACE NAMES from the Gaelic ***àird*** meaning *promontory* or *point*. So **Ardbeg**: little headland; **Ardmore**: big point.

aroon around

Arthur's Seat The big hill rising in the centre of Edinburgh, an extinct volcano close to the Scottish parliament.

ashet NORTH EAST large, oval serving plate

ask for → **Fiona was asking for you** Fiona was asking *after* you, was asking how you were; it's not that Fiona wanted you.

at that

In spoken Scots the *th* often disappears.
ats nae right that's not right
izzat right?
at beats everything

athoot NORTH EAST without

ye canna gin oot athoot a jaikit

athort OLDER SCOTS across

auch IN PLACE NAMES from the Gaelic ***achadh*** meaning *field.* So **Auchenshuggle**: field of rye.

auchter IN PLACE NAMES from the Gaelic ***uachdar*** meaning *high land* or *upper part*. So **Auchermuchty**: upland area where pigs are kept.

aul, auld old

Auld Alliance This is the name given to the long-standing friendship between Scotland and France (traditionally in a joint stand against England). In the past it was documented in treaties lending support in various ways (the original treaties being dated October 1295) with links being forged both politically and through marriage. Nowadays it has lost its political importance and is used in a more general sense.

auld lang syne long long ago

The song by Robert Burns is one of Scotland's gifts to the world and has become an international standard. The whole poem is hardly ever sung in its entirety. The following two verses and chorus will stand you in good stead.

Should auld acquaintance be
forgot,
And never brought to mind?
Should auld acquaintance be
forgot,
And auld lang syne?

Chorus

For auld lang syne, my dear,
For auld lang syne,
We'll tak a cup o' kindness yet,
For auld lang syne.

last verse

And there's a hand, my trusty fiere!
And gies a hand o' thine!
And we'll tak a right gude-willie waught,
For auld lang syne

Chorus

For auld lang syne etc.

fiere friend
tak a right gude-willie waught take a good old swig or two

Auld Reekie Edinburgh, the old smoky place

auld-farrant OLDER SCOTS old-fashioned, old-style

ava NORTH EAST at all
nae use ava no use at all

aw all

awa away
come awa, quinie come on, girl

In the North East **awa** can also mean *dead.*

away

A basic word in the Scots vocabulary, with a wide range of uses, such as:

away oot and get some milk from the Spar will you go out and get some milk from the Spar
away! not three thousand! *expresses surprise and disbelief*
away raffle yerself! don't be silly!
come away in come on in
that you away hame? are you going home?

Confusion can arise from one particular use.

is Dougie in there with you? – no, he's away

The answer means:
no, Dougie has just left

but is puzzling to non-Scots speakers, who are more likely to understand the answer as meaning:
no, Dougie is absent
or: no, Dougie's on holiday
or: no, Dougie's travelling on business

and who might even reply with:

no, he's not away, I saw him down the corridor just ten minutes ago so causing at best bewilderment, at worst an argument.

ay IN PLACE NAMES a common ending, from the Norse ***ey*** or ***øy*** meaning island. So **Pabbay**: priest's island.

ay of

aye

Three main meanings to this core Scots word:

1) yes

2) hello
aye aye hello

3) OLDER SCOTS always; still
he wis aye there, sitting by the fire

Aye can also be used as a tag word at the end of a question to show that the person asking the question expects the answer to be *yes*.
you'll bring them back the morra aye? you'll bring them back tomorrow, won't you?

And there's also:
aye night one night

and
Yours aye a slightly old-fashioned but common conclusion to a letter: yours ever

ayont OLDER SCOTS beyond

ayre SHETLAND beach

B

babby baby, a sentimentalized word

bachle little man, insignificant little man (not to be confused with **bauchle**)

back → **at the back of seven** just after seven o'clock, maybe five or ten minutes past. Interestingly, there is no corresponding expression for the time just before the hour.

back close the back part of the common entrance to a block of flats

baffies slippers

bag off SLANG get off with someone **by the end of the party everybody had bagged off, except me** by the end of the party everybody had got themselves a partner, except me

baggie 1) minnow 2) NORTH EAST (little) bag

bahookie SLANG backside, butt

bairen NORTH EAST child, baby

bairn child

> This can also be used as a verb.
> **he bairned her** he made her pregnant

baith both

balloch IN PLACE NAMES from the Gaelic ***bealach*** meaning *pass*.

ballop flies (*on trousers*)

bal IN PLACE NAMES from the Gaelic ***baile*** meaning *village*. So **Ballachulish**: village on the narrows.

Balmoral Castle The royal castle between Braemar and Ballater in Deeside, still the summer holiday residence of the Queen and royal family, was a favourite resort of Queen Victoria and Prince Albert, who oversaw building work in 1855.

bam SLANG short for **bampot**, crazy person **put that doon, ye bam!** put that down, you idiot!

bampot SLANG lunatic

bammy SLANG crazy

banjo SLANG This can be used as a verb, meaning *to hit*.

the wee lassie banjoed him wi her handbag

bank notes Scottish banks still issue their own notes (there are three types: Clydesdale, Bank of Scotland and Royal Bank of Scotland). The one-pound note, now extinct in England, still lives on in Scotland. Internationally, Scottish bank notes still have some way to go to achieve full recognition and travellers from Scotland may have problems changing Scottish notes abroad.

banks-broo SHETLAND cliff edge

Bannockburn (Battle of) In this battle, which took place in June 1314, Robert I of Scotland (Robert the Bruce) defeated Edward II of England. It proved to be decisive in the Scottish Wars of Independence and eventually led to the signing of the Treaty of Edinburgh, which recognized Scotland's independence. A visitor centre now marks the battle site near Stirling.

bap NORTH EAST a soft roll

bar IN PLACE NAMES from the Gaelic ***bàrr*** meaning *top* or *height*. So **Dunbar**: fort of the height.

Barras (Barrows) a Glasgow market, a source of cheap CDs, DVDs, clothes and some antiques

barry EAST COAST SLANG great, brilliant, fantastic, beautiful

Bass Rock A volcanic plug rising to over 100 metres out of the Firth of Forth. Home to the hermit St Baldred in the 9th century, it became a state prison in the 17th, was occupied for three years from 1691 by **Jacobites**, and is now of world importance to ornithologists as home to a major gannet colony and other seabirds.

bauchle old, worn-out shoe

baw 1) ball 2) cry

that kid is bawin its eyes oot

baw-faced SLANG with a round, chubby face. In context this is often used like **bawheid** to imply that the person with the round face is a bit of an idiot.

bawheid SLANG This is literally a person with a big round face, something which the Scots find amusing and worthy of a special term. It's normally used as a fairly cheeky form of address.
whit ye dae that fur, ye great glaikit bawheid! what'd you do that for, you

stupid great fathead!

beamer → **to get a beamer** to go red in the face

beauty → **ya beauty!** great! brilliant!

bed recess an alcove, usually in the kitchen of a traditional tenement flat, which was formerly used as a sleeping area; often repurposed these DIY days as a cosy dining space

been NORTH EAST also: bone

beet NORTH EAST boot

beg IN PLACE NAMES from the Gaelic ***beag*** meaning little. So **Inverbeg**: little river mouth.

ben[1] IN PLACE NAMES from the Gaelic ***beinn*** meaning *mountain* or *hill.* So **Ben Wyvis**: huge mountain; **Benbecula**: hill of the fords.

ben[2]

A preposition meaning *in* or *into* but which is not quite so easy to tie down

to a single English equivalent.
come ben the house come on in
away ben and fetch ma... go into the next room and fetch my...
come on ben the sitting room come into the sitting room
he went ben the back of the hoose he went through to the back of the house
she went ben the house This doesn't mean that she went into the house, but that she went into another room.

bendy juice SLANG alcohol

ben end the inner room of a **but and ben** cottage

Ben Nevis At 4406 feet or 1344 metres, this is Scotland's and Britain's highest mountain (but not the most spectacular).

bere NORTH EAST [pronounced BARE] barley

berkie → SLANG **to throw a berkie** to go beserk; to have a fit

berren NORTH EAST child; children; otherwise written as **bairn(s)**

Bertie Auld RHYMING SLANG cold

The 1960s Celtic football star has entered the world of rhyming slang.
bit Bertie Auld in this room, eh?

besom an annoying or unpleasant woman

bevvied up drunk

bevvy drink

fancy a wee bevvy? fancy a drink?
they've been oot on the bevvy they've been out drinking

bevvy-merchant drinker

Bhoys Celtic football players

bide NORTH EAST 1) stay 2) live

This is old or very literary in southern English but still in everyday use in North East Scotland.
you go then, I'm biding here you go then, I'm staying here
is this far Hector bides? is this where Hector lives?

bidie-in an unmarried partner (particularly female) living in the same house

big yin big one; big person

A friendly way of addressing someone who the speaker sees as being taller (or more important) than himself. Billy Connolly is known in Glasgow as the Big Yin.

bigg SHETLAND build

biggin building; house

bile boil

Billy(-boy) SLANG derogatory for Protestant

birk NORTH EAST birch tree. The word is nowadays known to most Scots through association with the Burns song 'The Birks o' Aberfeldy'.

birl whirl, swing

> **if a lassie goes to a ceilidh she must expect to be birled about**

bit This can also mean *place, house.*

> **we all went back tae his bit for a bevvy**

bittick NORTH EAST OLDER SCOTS a little bit

bittie → NORTH EAST **a bittie** a bit, a little

black house Made of turf, with a roof of thatch or moss, no chimney, an open peat fire inside, they were found mainly in the Western Highlands.

black-affronted absolutely mortified
I was black-affronted I could've died with embarrassment

blaeberry bilberry

blair IN PLACE NAMES from the Gaelic ***blàr*** meaning *plain* or *open land.* So **Blairgowrie**: goat plain.

blate NORTH EAST OLDER SCOTS shy

blaw blow

bleed NORTH EAST also the noun: blood

bleezin NORTH EAST SLANG drunk, smashed, plastered

bleish of rain NORTH EAST downpour

blended A blended is a whisky made from the output of more than one distillery, as contrasted with a **single malt**.

blether This can be a verb and a noun.
she's a right wee blether she's a proper little chatterbox
we had a good blether we had a good old chat
what's that damn woman blethering on about now?

blin blind

blin drift NORTH EAST drifting snow; heavy snowfall; driving blizzard

blyde SHETLAND glad

blythe OLDER SCOTS contented; a variant of **blyde**, but only really encountered in literary works

boaby SLANG willie, penis

boak vomit
it gies me the boak it makes me sick
he gies me the dry boak he makes me absolutely sick

bodie → **a bodie** you, people

a bodie needs someone to talk to

boggin SLANG stinking; disgusting

bogy → **the game's a bogy** the game's up, it's all over, you might as well forget it, it'll never work

boil → SLANG **away boil yer heid** go away; don't give me that nonsense; don't be stupid

boiling a boiled sweet

boke same as **boak**

bonnet any hat, especially a flat hat

bonnie pretty, beautiful
bonnie sair pretty sore

bonspiel curling match

bonxie SHETLAND great skua

bosie NORTH EAST 1) cuddle 2) bosom
och, come to mammy for a bosie let mummy cuddle it better

bothie This is a mountain or forest hut where walkers can stop for the night (just walk in and leave it as you found it, or better). No booking, no keys. Bothies are basic, one up from a tent. You might find a wood-burning stove, but don't expect furniture or cutlery. And in place of a loo, you'll find a shovel.
The word *bothie* can also be used for a hut on a building site or a rest room, say, for bus drivers.

bottlin Just before a girl is going to get married, her friends might get her dressed up and take her through the streets or around the offices or around the shop floor, inviting passing men to have a kiss from the bride-to-be in exchange for a small sum of money (useful for wedding presents). This is a pretty raucous custom, involving a lot of singing and tin-banging and tambourine-shaking, a bit alarming for those who don't know what's going on, and, not really surprisingly, it's on the way out in the modern world.

bowf bark

bowfin disgusting

bowly SLANG [bow pronounced to rhyme with COW] bowlegged

boy

Can mean a **man** when used to refer to a labourer; so a stonemason might say:

I could'nae get the boys tae come oot oan a public holiday

bra OLDER SCOTS good; brave

brack NORTH EAST dark fruit loaf

brae hill

The word is originally Gaelic, ***bràigh*** meaning *hillside* or *slope*. So **Braemar**: the upper part of Mar.

Braemar Gathering Annual **highland games** held in September and traditionally attended by members of the Royal Family.

brammle NORTH EAST blackberry

brar brother

braw good; great

bread IN PLACE NAMES from the Gaelic ***braghaid*** meaning *heights*. So **Breadalbane**: the upper part of Alba (Alba being the Gaelic for Scotland).

bree 1) liquid 2) broth 3) GLASGOW brother

breeks trousers; pants

breeng → **smoke came breenging in** the smoke came rushing in

breether NORTH EAST brother

brick → **in wi the bricks** If you are **in wi the bricks**, you are a long-serving employee, part of the furniture.

old Jamie thought he wis in wi the bricks, till he had a chat wi the boss last week

brig bridge

brikks trousers; pants

Brittonic one of the old Celtic languages

broo dole, unemployment benefit

brosey NORTH EAST big, burly, strapping

bruaich IN PLACE NAMES from the Gaelic ***bruthach*** meaning *hill*. So **Tighnabruaich**: house on the hill.

bruck SHETLAND rubbish

bubbliejock OLDER SCOTS a turkey

buckie 1) whelk 2) **Buckie**, short for Buckfast®, fortified wine

bunker a kitchen cabinet

bunnet variant of bonnet, hat

burden LEGAL SCOTS A burden is a restriction on the use of land or property.

burn stream

Burns' Night The birthday of Scotland's national poet is celebrated across the country on 25 January every year. This traditionally takes the form of a Burns' Supper where **haggis, neeps** and **tatties** are eaten. There may also be poetry readings, singing and a **ceilidh**.

burroo dole

on the burroo on the dole, receiving unemployment benefit

but

In Scots this can be positioned at

the end of a sentence to act as an emphasizer.
that's really great but! that's just really great!
this is no place to be in winter but! this is definitely no place to be in winter!
you found me quick but! you found me pretty quick, didn't you!

but and ben a home consisting of just a kitchen and a living room, usually a cottage

but end NORTH EAST the outer room or kitchen of a **but and ben** cottage

buttery a croissant-like roll from the North East

button up → **d'ye think ma heid buttons up the back?** do you think I'm stupid?

bygaun → NORTH EAST OLDER SCOTS **in the bygaun** by the way

byke wasps' nest

byoch NORTH EAST belch

C

caa NORTH EAST call

caald SHETLAND cold

caddy lamb SHETLAND pet lamb

cairn IN PLACE NAMES from the Gaelic ***càrn*** meaning a *rocky hill* (as well as the sense of a pile of stones marking a summit). So **Cairngorm**: blue hill.

cal NORTH EAST cold

caller NORTH EAST fresh

came → **she has came** Use of the preterite instead of the past participle is common in speech.

can

> In some regions (mainly the north) you'll still hear variant uses.
> **I'll can dae it the morn** I'll be able to do it tomorrow
> **I might can help ye** I might be able to help you

cannae can't

canny sly, astute; (*with money*) careful

cantation NORTH EAST OLDER SCOTS discussion; dialogue

cappie NORTH EAST an ice-cream cone

carry-out take-away; a meal or some drinks to take away; a place that sells food to take away

> **we could get a carry-out and go back to my place**
> **there used to be a Chinese carry-out round here**

cartoon NORTH EAST In the North East a **cartoon** can be used to mean a *carton,* as in a carton of milk.

case → **he's been gettin on my case** he's been getting on my nerves, annoying me

catched NORTH EAST caught

cauld cold

caunle candle

caur tram; car

ceilidh [pronounced **kay**-lee] There'll be a band playing traditional Scottish music with fiddle and accordion and drums (or possibly some or all of these replaced by a Yamaha), Scottish dancing, tables and chairs set out around the room. And drink and food. (Traditionally, a ceilidh was a night spent telling stories and singing songs around a peat fire in Gaelic-speaking communities.)

Celtic Connections [pronounced Keltic, not Seltic (which is the football team)] Annual festival held in Glasgow early in the year which celebrates Celtic and traditional music from Scotland and around the world (includes concerts, workshops, masterclasses and competitions).

ceud mìle fàilte [pronounced kee-ut meel-ih **faal**tchuh] Gaelic for one hundred thousand welcomes

chaave struggle

chaavin awa NORTH EAST OK, not bad. This is a typical response to the question **fit like?**

chaff chat

chaffin awa NORTH EAST working away, working hard; see also **chaavin awa**

champit mashed

chap knock

chap the door knock at the door

if I'm in Partick the morrow I'll come by and chap your door I'll come round to visit

chappit mashed

chaumer NORTH EAST room

cheeper kiss, peck

chib 1) stab; slash 2) knife; weapon

chiel guy, fellow

chipper NORTH EAST fish and chip shop; in other parts of Scotland it is known as a

chippie. The word can also mean *fish and chips.*

> **we picked up a chipper on the way back from the beach**

chippie a fish and chip shop

chitter NORTH EAST shiver

chittery bite NORTH EAST a small snack eaten after swimming to stop you from shivering

chookie SLANG idiot

chookie bird tweetie-pie, little bird (as used by an adult talking to a little child)

chorie SLANG thieve
to be on the chorie to be thieving, to be a thief

choryin spree SLANG thieving expedition

chowie chew

chowk NORTH EAST cheek

chuckies NORTH EAST pebbles

chuddie chewing gum

chuffing awa NORTH EAST same as **chaavin awa**

chum

> In Scots this can also be used to form a verb.
> **I'll chum you intae town** I'll go into town with you to keep you company

he chummed her back to the station

clachan IN PLACE NAMES a Gaelic word meaning *village*

claethes clothes

claik OLDER SCOTS talk

clamjamfry mess, odds and ends, clutter

Clan system The word *clan* comes from the Gaelic ***clann*** meaning *family* or *children* and most members of a clan will share a common descent. However, not all people with the same surname necessarily belong to the same (or any) clan. Clans were more established in the Highlands and islands than in the Lowlands and were headed by the chief who also acted as judge in legal disputes and would call upon his men to follow him into battle when the need arose. The land the clan lived on was owned by the chief and the main wealth derived from it came from cattle. In the 18th century and particularly as a result of measures imposed after the battle of **Culloden**, the power wielded by the clans diminished.

clap pat; stroke

clappie NORTH EAST pat; stroke
gie the horsie a wee clappie, he'll no hurt ye give the horse a little pat, he won't hurt you

clarsach a traditional Celtic harp, smaller than a classical harp but not as small as a lap harp

clartit NORTH EAST caked, covered (in mud, make-up etc)

clarty, clatty dirty

Clearances In the late 18th and early 19th century landowners in the Highlands and islands discovered that they could make more money from rearing sheep on their land than they could from the tenants who had been working the same land for generations. The tenants were (often forcibly) evicted from their homes. Poverty, combined with the famine of 1846, led many to emigrate to Australia and North America.

cleg horsefly

close

common entrance and stairwell of a tenement block; everybody who lives off that staircase
the whole close could hear him

coming home
yer up the wrang close there you're barking up the wrong tree there

cludgie SLANG loo; john

Clyde → **I've no just come up the Clyde in a banana boat** I'm not stupid, not naive

clype tell tales
you wee clype, you! you telltale!

coin NORTH EAST a less common spelling of **quine**

come over → NORTH EAST **there's nothing coming over me** there's nothing wrong with me

Common Ridings These events take place in various towns in the Borders over the summer. Groups of horsemen ride around the boundaries of the town. The ceremonies date back to the time when the Border regions were disputed land and had to be defended.

coo cow

cookie-mouthed EAST COAST fond of eating biscuits and buns

coorse NORTH EAST 1) coarse 2) difficult

Corbett any Scottish mountain over 2,500

feet (762m) and under 3,000 feet (915m)

corrie-fisted left-handed

coup[1] [pronounced COWP] 1) rubbish tip 2) mess
see his room, some coup eh? his room's a right mess

coup[2] 1) knock over 2) fall over
so he stands up and coups his biryani all ower her dress

coupon SLANG 1) face 2) head

> **ah've got a sair coupon**

Court of Session LEGAL SCOTS the Scottish supreme civil court, sitting in Edinburgh

couthie twee

cowk NORTH EAST retch

cowking → NORTH EAST SLANG **I was cowking when Aberdeen lost** I was sick when Aberdeen lost

cowp same as **coup**

craa SHETLAND hooded crow

crabbit bad-tempered; morose; surly

crack chat; good conversation

> **all five of us spent the night in the pub, it was good crack**
>
> Also a verb:
>
> **ah cracked wi the barman a while aboot...**

In the North East this is also used to mean *to strike* as in **to crack a spunk** (strike a match).

craic another spelling of **crack**, the noun

craig OLDER SCOTS neck

crannie NORTH EAST little finger

craw → **shoot the craw** SLANG leave, go away, scarper, do a runner

craw-stepped gable a traditional Scots architectural feature

cream puff → RHYMING SLANG **take the cream puff** go into a huff, get offended

creamer NORTH EAST 1) an ice-cream shop 2) an ice-cream van

creelin same as a **bottlin**

croft small farm, small holding

Crown Office LEGAL SCOTS the Scottish office responsible for the prosecution of crime

crunk her up! NORTH EAST SLANG get a

move on!, hurry up!

crunk her up, ah've nae got a' day!

cry also means *to call*
cry it what ye like call it what you like
what d'ye cry that instrument he's playing?

cuddie horse

Cuillins mountains on Skye

Culloden This battle took place in 1746 between the **Jacobites** under Bonnie Prince Charlie and the Hanoverians under the Duke of Cumberland. The terrain – open moorland near Inverness – was unsuited to the Jacobites' style of fighting and they suffered a huge defeat in what was the last pitched battle on British soil.

curn → **a curn...** a few...

cutty sark OLDER SCOTS a short, woman's shirt

D

da[1] dad

da[2] SHETLAND the

da[3] NORTH EAST don't
da ken dunno
da hae time don't have time

I da agree I don't agree

dae do

dal IN PLACE NAMES from the Gaelic ***dail*** meaning *field* or *dale*. So **Dalkeith**: field of the wood, wood field.

dan SHETLAND then

Dan SLANG derogatory for Catholic

darg work; day's work

dat SHETLAND that

daunder, dauner stroll

de SHETLAND you

In Shetland the word **du** for *you* has different case endings, like a Germanic or Scandinavian language.
dat is fir de that's for you

dear green place Glasgow

Declaration of Arbroath A Latin document written in 1320 asserting Scotland's claim for independence from England and its right to freedom. Bearing the seals of Scottish earls and barons, it was sent to Pope John XXII. The Declaration of Arbroath served as a model for the American Declaration of Independence.

dee 1) die 2) NORTH EAST do

Dee → NORTH EAST **ah've nae just come**

doon the Dee on a digestive I'm not stupid, wasn't born yesterday. This is a parallel to the Glaswegian expression about the **Clyde** and banana boats.

deek EAST COAST SLANG look at; look; see
deek that wee gadgie in the kilt look at that little guy in the kilt
ah cannae deek ony change I can't see any change
Also a noun.
take a deek at this video take a look at this video

deem NORTH EAST girl

deep-fried Mars® Bar a Scottish invention, affectionately known as **angina-on-a-plate**

deid [pronounced DEED] dead

deif [pronounced DEEF] deaf

depute In administrative language a **depute** is the equivalent of a *deputy.*

the Depute Director of Parks

Desperate Dan As well as being the name of a well-known cartoon character, this is also used to refer to a large-format steak and kidney pie.

deuk SHETLAND a duck

dicht wipe; clean

didgy SLANG dustbin

didna, didnae didn't

ding doon pelt down

> **with the rain dingin doon**

dinger → SLANG **to go yer dinger**
1) to be very energetic 2) to be very angry; also used with the verb *do* or **dae** or **dee**
he's deen his dinger the day he's really going for it today
wi the wee dug's tail daein its dinger at ye like that ye have to give in
when the little dog's tail wags away at you like that, you have to give in

dingy SLANG ignore

> **ah did ask but ye jist dingied me**

dinnae don't

dippet SLANG daft, stupid

direction OLDER SCOTS This can also mean *address* in North Eastern usage.

dirk the traditional Highlandman's dagger

dirl NORTH EAST noise

> **keep yer dirl doon!**

dirler 1) In the Glasgow area a **dirler** is a person who sings mouth music.
2) In the North East a **dirler** is a toilet.

disnae doesn't

dispone LEGAL SCOTS To **dispone** land or

property is to transfer ownership of it.

div NORTH EAST do
I div like... I do like...

diznae doesn't

dizzen OLDER SCOTS dozen

dochter OLDER SCOTS daughter

dock NORTH EAST SLANG bottom, bum

dod piece, dollop

a big dod of cream

doh → **up to high doh** very worried; nervous; in a state of great excitement

dolly dimple RHYMING SLANG simple, simple-minded

dominie NORTH EAST OLDER SCOTS schoolmaster

Donald any Scottish mountain south of the **Highland line** that is more than 2,000 feet (610m)

Donald RHYMING SLANG short for **Donald Duck**, which means *luck*

Dons → **the Dons** nickname for Aberdeen Football Club

doo dove

dook soak
to go for a dook to go for a swim
to dook for apples to try to get apples out of a bucket of water using your teeth

– an old Halloween game

dookers swimming trunks

dooket 1) dovecote 2) pigeonhole

doolie fool

doon down

doot same as **doubt**

Doric Doric is the distinctive Scots language of north-east Scotland, particularly of Aberdeen and its surrounding region.

doss SLANG stupid

dottled NORTH EAST confused

doubt

> In Scots this also means *to expect* or *to think* – the exact opposite of *doubt.* (French has a similar construction in *se douter* = to suspect).
>
> **I doubt ye've got a wrang number** I think you've got the wrong number
>
> **I doubt ye're richt** I expect you're right

douce gentle; refined

dour IN PLACE NAMES from the old Gaelic ***dobhar*** meaning *water.* So **Aberdour**: mouth of the river Dour.

dout[1] cigarette end

dout[2] NORTH EAST go to **doubt**

downie continental quilt

dowp NORTH EAST backside, bottom

dram a drink of whisky, no longer a specific measure though

> **fancy a wee dram before the hearse gets here, Archie?**

drap drop

dreich [pronounced DREECH with the CH as in loch] grey and dismal

> **one more dreich weekend like this and that's me aff tae Barcelona**

drookit, droukit soaked, drenched

drouth NORTH EAST 1) drinker 2) thirst 3) dryness

drouthy thirsty

drum IN PLACE NAMES from the Gaelic ***druim*** meaning *ridge*. So **Drummore**: big ridge; **Drumnadrochit**: ridge bridge.

drumlie murky (*water, liquid*)

dry stane dyke dry-stone wall

du SHETLAND you

> Shetland retains the distinctions of different words for *you*, that exist in other European languages, but which have long since disappeared in English. In Shetland the word *you* is either reserved for people seen as social superiors or it is just the plural form of **du**.

dubbie muddy

dubs mud; puddles

dug dog

dum, dun IN PLACE NAMES from the Gaelic ***dùn*** meaning *fortress* or *mound*. So **Dumbarton**: fortress of the Britons; **Dunblane**: St Blane's hill; **Dunkeld**: fort of the Caledonians.

dumfounert dumbfounded, stunned

dun IN PLACE NAMES same as **dum**

dunnie 1) cellar 2) the passageway of the **back close**, which is low down and dark

dunt a heavy blow

he got the dunt NORTH EAST he got the sack

dunter SHETLAND eider duck

Dux At school the **Dux** is the pupil with the highest overall marks in the top year.

dwaam, dwam → **to be away in a dwaam** to be in a dream, to be in a daze

dy SHETLAND your
tak du dy time you take your time

dyke a wall, as around a field

E

eccle IN PLACE NAMES from the Gaelic ***eaglais*** meaning *church*. So **Ecclefechan**: church of St Beachan.

edin IN PLACE NAMES from the Gaelic ***aodann*** meaning *slope*. So (possibly) **Edinburgh**: fortress on the hill.

Edinburgh Scotland's capital city and location of many of the country's most important historical, political and cultural institutions, including the new Scottish parliament (window detail illustrated). Edinburgh plays host to a fair **wheen** of festivals, including **Edinburgh International Book**

Festival, in August every year, **Edinburgh International Jazz and Blues Festival**, July/August, the **Edinburgh Festival** the famous annual arts festival showcasing some of the top orchestras and theatre companies from around the world, end August-September and the **Edinburgh Military Tattoo** which runs for several weeks over the summer with marching pipebands, dancing and fireworks.

ee OLDER SCOTS eye; note the unusual plural form: **een**

eedjit idiot

eela SHETLAND sea-angling

een 1) one 2) OLDER SCOTS eyes

eence once

eeran → NORTH EAST **tae rin an eeran** to go shopping, to do the shopping

eerans NORTH EAST shopping

eese NORTH EAST use
nae eese ava no use at all

effeiring to LEGAL SCOTS pertaining to

efter after
see you efter after what? after nothing; just means *see you later, see you*

efterneen NORTH EAST afternoon

Embra the capital city of Scotland

erra GLASGOW rendering of *there's a*

erse NORTH EAST arse
ah couldna be ersed SLANG I couldn't be bothered, couldn't be arsed

ess NORTH EAST SHETLAND ashes

essikert SHETLAND refuse vehicle, bin lorry

expede LEGAL SCOTS draw up

eywis always

F

fa NORTH EAST who

factor LEGAL SCOTS Some Scottish flats have a manager or a company who is paid to look after repairs, painting of common parts etc. This **factor** tends to have a reputation for not getting things done.

fae NORTH EAST from

fæder SHETLAND father

Fair The last two weeks in July in Glasgow are known as the **Fair**. It's a traditional time for holidays (especially in the older industrial days).

fairly that NORTH EAST right enough

fairm farm

fairmer farmer

fairt SHETLAND scared

faither father

fan NORTH EAST when

fancy piece NORTH EAST

> In the North East of Scotland a woman wouldn't be at all bothered about her man having a **fancy piece**. She might even offer him one. It's a cake.

fankle mess; tangle

yer cables are all fankled up your cables are all tangled up

> **he got himself into a right fankle with question 3 in his maths test**

fantoosh OLDER SCOTS flashy

far[1] NORTH EAST where

far ye fae? where are you from?

far[2] → **I could see her far enough** I can't stand her; I can't be bothered with her

fash bother, upset

dinna fash yersel This has differing shades of meaning: don't worry about it; don't get angry, don't be annoyed

feart afraid

feartie coward

fecht OLDER SCOTS fight

feck NORTH EAST OLDER SCOTS majority

feel NORTH EAST This is also used as an adjective: *daft, silly.* Or as a noun: *fool.*

fell highly

fell muckle OLDER SCOTS enormous

fend NORTH EAST effort, attempt

fergie combine harvester (because made by Massey Ferguson)

fey OLDER SCOTS [pronounced FAY] doomed

fi from

ficher NORTH EAST OLDER SCOTS tinker, fiddle

> **ah'll hae a ficher aboot wi the engine**

fiere OLDER SCOTS friend

fin NORTH EAST when (*conjunction, for indirect questions*)

find → **she didn't have her troubles to find** she had a lot of troubles, she wasn't short of troubles

fine NORTH EAST

> This has a slightly different usage in Aberdeenshire – it is much more positive. If you ask someone whether they enjoyed their day off and they reply that **it was fine**, that means that it was lovely rather than just OK.
>
> **she's a fine quine** This is most commonly used to mean *she's a friendly woman.*

fine well very well

you know fine well what I mean you know very well what I mean

first-foot To **first-foot** someone is to visit them first thing in the New Year, maybe just after midnight or maybe a little later, on New Year's Day. First-footers will traditionally be made welcome and given a drink or two.

let's go round and first-foot the Macleods

fiscal LEGAL SCOTS short for **procurator fiscal**, a Scottish public prosecutor

fish supper fish and chips. It's not usual in Scotland to specify the type of fish or to offer a choice. If you want fish without the chips, ask for a **single fish**.

fistle NORTH EAST rummage

fit[1] NORTH EAST what

fit[2] → NORTH EAST **fit like?** how are you?
fit ye daein? what are you doing?
fit div ye wint? what do you want?

fit wye NORTH EAST 1) why 2) how
fit wye nae? why not?
fit a stoater! that's brilliant!
fit wye can I help you? how can I help you?

fitba football

fitna een NORTH EAST which one

fizz → **he had a face like fizz** he looked very angry

flair floor

flechie NORTH EAST flea-bitten

flee SHETLAND fishing fly

fleein SLANG drunk

fleg NORTH EAST startle; scare

flit move house (*also Northern English*)

flite scold

flitting move (from one home to another)

flooer flower

flunky SLANG condom

fly NORTH EAST same as a **fly cup**

fly cup NORTH EAST cup of tea or coffee; the word **fly** no longer has any separate meaning; the cup of tea or coffee will be neither quick nor taken in a furtive manner

fly half a quick half pint of beer (as well as the rugby position)

flyting quarrel; slanging match

foo NORTH EAST how
foo mony? how many?
foo ye daein'? how are you doing?
foo aul are ye? how old are you?

fool NORTH EAST In the North East this can also mean *dirty*.

fool mochit NORTH EAST filthy dirty

foosty 1) smelly, like an old room
2) NORTH EAST mouldy

footer fiddle

> **painting in behind the pipes is a terrible footer**

footery fiddly

for → **what are ye for?** what would you like?, as said in a bar, for example

forby(e) OLDER SCOTS also; besides
forby(e) that moreover; apart from that

forenoon late morning

forfochen OLDER SCOTS done in, exhausted

forjeskit exhausted

forkietail SHETLAND NORTH EAST earwig

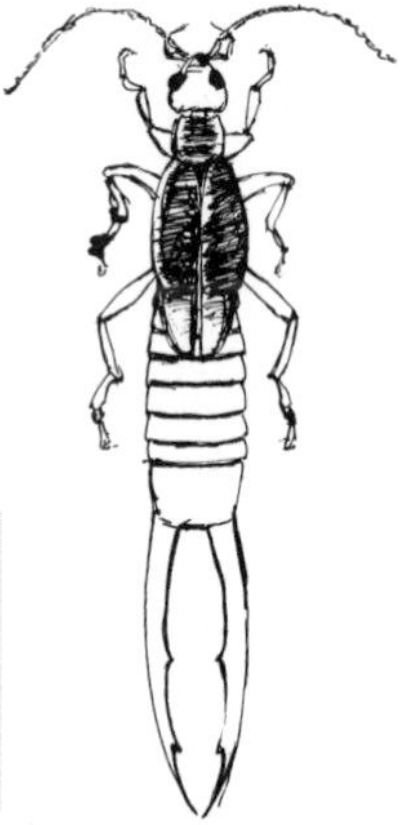

fou OLDER SCOTS drunk

foushty, fousty NORTH EAST mouldy

fowk NORTH EAST people, folk

foy SHETLAND party

Fringe An annual Edinburgh arts festival which takes place over 3 weeks in August/

September, attracting thousands of performers from all over the UK and abroad, who stage shows of all conceivable types in venues large and small.

frush NORTH EAST OLDER SCOTS tender, sensitive

fu 1) full 2) drunk)3 NORTH EAST how
fu is du? SHETLAND how are you?

fuil NORTH EAST fool
gang fuil go crazy

fur rendering of *for*

fur coat n nae knickers all for show, superficial, flashy

furth of outside

the Burns museum lies furth of the capital city

fyles NORTH EAST sometimes

G

gad! NORTH EAST yuck!

gadge SLANG guy
the ticket gadge the ticket man

gadgie NORTH EAST man, guy
a gallus wee gadgie a tough little character

gads NORTH EAST yuck

gaed NORTH EAST gave; given

Gaelic [pronounced GALLic] Scots Gaelic is closely related to Irish and more distantly to Welsh and has an estimated 60,000 speakers (out of a total Scottish population of some 5 million). It came into Scotland from the 4th century onwards, flowing in with the immigrant Irish. Place name evidence suggests that at least some Gaelic was once spoken all over Scotland, probably between 500 and 1000 BC, but it was gradually ousted by the Scots spoken in and around the developing capital of Edinburgh. In the later Middle Ages, the language became increasingly identified with the West Highlands and Western Isles. These are the main Gaelic-speaking parts of Scotland today. Here you'll find road signs in English and Gaelic, and television and radio also offer a few Gaelic programmes. But even in communities where Gaelic is the main language you won't come across anyone who is not bilingual in English.
Some basic Gaelic phrases are given on pages 154-155

gaet SHETLAND path

gallus 1) tough 2) cocky 3) brilliant, great

galluses braces (*for trousers*)

gammon the same as *ham* in England

gan NORTH EAST going
hud gan keep going

gang OLDER SCOTS go

gansey SHETLAND jersey

gash SLANG rubbish, crap

gaun going

geggie SLANG mouth
shut yer geggie shut your mouth

gemme [pronounced GAME] game

gemmie SLANG brilliant

gen up? SLANG is that right?

Gers Rangers football team

get → **I'll get you down the road** not a threat, this means I'll walk down the road with you

gey [pronounced: GUY] very
gey cauld the nicht, eh? pretty cold tonight, eh?

ghillie shoes traditional leather shoes worn with the kilt

gie give

gies give us
dinnae gies that crap don't give us that crap

gieza... can I have...?

This is a common way of asking for something in a shop or bar; it sounds abrupt to the non-Scots ear but isn't perceived as rude.

gin OLDER SCOTS if; you're only likely to come across this nowadays in songs or poems

ging NORTH EAST go

ginger GLASGOW any fizzy soft drink

girdle griddle; for cooking pancakes and the like on

girn whine

girnie Someone who is **girnie** is alway whining about something. It's often used for a baby, who just feels like a good whine about things.

girse NORTH EAST grass

glaikit stupid, gormless

Glasgow Scotland's largest city with an industrial heritage of heavy engineering and shipbuilding on the Clyde and trade with the colonies in the late 18th century, notably the importation of tobacco and sugar. Despite a decline in heavy industry, the city has experienced a revival in fortunes and is now a major retail and business centre with a highly developed sense of self-promotion. A place where people talk to people.

Glasgow Fair This is a traditional two-week July holiday in Glasgow, when factories would shut and you'd take your holidays then (whether it suited or no).

glaur [pronounced to rhyme with FLOOR] mud

gleikit same as **glaikit**

Glencoe In 1691 the government of William and Mary demanded that **Jacobite** clan chiefs sign an oath of allegiance. The chief of the Macdonalds of Glencoe was late in doing so and this was seen as a pretext for action against them. A regiment belonging to the Campbell Earl of Argyle was dispatched to Glencoe where the Macdonalds were obliged to offer them hospitality. Shortly afterwards the commander of the regiment received orders that all Macdonalds under 70 were to be put to the sword. The massacre took place in February 1692. Thirty-eight of the clan were killed, including the chief, and more died trying to escape over the mountains.

This massacre has gone down in history as the Campbells wreaking revenge on their old enemies the Macdonalds when in fact they were following orders which came from the King himself.

glengarry a type of cap with a fold at the top running front to back and two strands of cloth hanging down at the back

Glesca Glasgow

Glesca screwdriver a hammer

Glesga Glasgow

Glesga kiss a head butt

Glesgie Glasgow

gloaming dusk

glottal stop

This is the characteristically Glaswegian omission of the 't' sound, making **buh-uh** out of *butter* and **beh-uh** out of *better.*

gluff SHETLAND fright

go can also mean *ride*
he nivver learnt tae go a bike he never learned to ride a bike

goat rendering of *got*

goldie → **a wee goldie** an affectionate expression for a glass of whisky

gonnae going to

> Also used to form typically Glaswegian requests.
> **gonnae gieza a fiver?** can you give me a fiver?
> **gonnae no say that!** please don't say that

goonie gown, nightdress

gooser NORTH EAST gooseberry

gow NORTH EAST OLDER SCOTS gull

gowk cuckoo

Graham any Scottish mountain between 2,000 feet and 2,500 feet (610-762m)

grain SHETLAND small amount

graip NORTH EAST fork, garden fork

graith OLDER SCOTS gear, tools, tackle; things

Granite City → **the Granite City** Aberdeen

gravat scarf

Great Glen This is the name given to the rift valley which runs from Inverness on the east coast to Fort William on the west coast. In 1822 the Caledonian Canal was built through the glen linking the Lochs Ness, Oich and Lochy and providing a navigable waterway from one side of Scotland to the other.

greet

Also means *cry, weep*
ach, dinna greet, hen, he'll be back
ah jist went hame n had a good greet

greeter someone who cries a lot; a cry-baby

greetin face SLANG jocular, but not terribly respectful, form of address. As seen at **bawface**, the Scots are fond of terms alluding to the shape and look of a person's face.
hey, greetin face, giezat hammer willya hey, chum, pass that hammer, eh?

greit same as **greet**

greive head farmworker

Gretna Green Just over the border from England, this small town became famous as the romantic destination for eloping couples trying to escape the tighter English marriage laws. Originally, in Scotland, a man and woman over the age of 16 could be married simply by declaring themselves husband and wife in front of witnesses. Nowadays a minister or authorized registrar must officiate but there are no stipulations regarding residence in the country and no parental consent is required for couples over 16.

grind SHETLAND gate

grip → NORTH EAST **he's such a grip** he's so tight with his money

grippie NORTH EAST tight, stingy, mean

growler NORTH EAST SLANG an ugly-looking woman; an old bag

grun NORTH EAST ground

gubbing defeat, often in a sports context
the under 15s got a right gubbing on Sunday, 35-3

gubful mouthful

guddle mess
seen his desk? what a guddle!

gude OLDER SCOTS good

guff NORTH EAST an English person

guffie NORTH EAST This is an English person. Either because of the Cockney habit of calling people *guv* or because of a tendency to talk a load of guff. Or maybe both.

guid good

guid kens SHETLAND god knows

guid... OLDER SCOTS ...in-law

guidman OLDER SCOTS husband

guiser A person, normally a child, who goes out **guising** at Halloween. The term also has special meaning at the annual **Up-Helly-Aa** festival. It involves squads of guisers parading around Lerwick, performing skits in the local halls, the burning of a replica Viking longship and general mayhem. The most important person in all this is the "Guiser Jarl" who leads the "Jarl Squad" who are all very elaborately dressed up as Vikings.

guising At Halloween children go out from door to door dressed up in fancy dress as witches, pirates, cowboys or anything you like, and, if invited in to a house, which is the custom, sing a song or tell a funny story, in exchange for some sweets or a little cash. Most people will have a special store of sweets and chocolate laid out in anticipation of the guising.

guizer same as **guiser**

guttered SLANG drunk

gutties trainers

gye same as **gey**

gype NORTH EAST SLANG idiot

H

haar NORTH EAST sea mist

hacker NORTH EAST As well as the standard meaning of a *computer hacker* this can also be 1) a smelly or repulsive person 2) an aggressive person.

hackit 1) ugly 2) NORTH EAST smelly, repulsive

haddy fool, twit (short for haddock)

haggis supper go to the **Menu Reader**

haill whole

haillie wholly

hairst SHETLAND autumn

hairy (Mary) GLASGOW a young girl, from teens to early twenties; a **hairy** is not going to be posh, it's not a flattering term

hak NORTH EAST search

> **hakkin aroon in the gorse for his golf ba**

hale jing bang NORTH EAST the whole lot

hale → NORTH EAST **it's hale watter** it's bucketing down, it's pouring with rain

half and half half a pint of beer and a

whisky

ham-and-egger NORTH EAST SLANG an incompetent, useless person

Hampden also **Hampden Park**, an international stadium (for football or rugby) in Glasgow

hand → NORTH EAST **to draw through hand** to go over, to talk over

hang → **to hang one on somebody** to hit somebody

happit covered

harl NORTH EAST To **harl** a wall is to roughcast it.

harling NORTH EAST roughcast

hashed NORTH EAST SLANG busy; in a hurry
ah'm gye hashed the day I'm very busy today
I cannae talk the noo, I'm hashed can't talk now, I'm in a rush

haud hold

hauf half

haugh IN PLACE NAMES a meadow by a river, from the Old English ***healh*** or ***halh*** meaning *corner* or *nook*. So: **Fleshers' Haugh** (on Glasgow Green, where Rangers first played).

haun hand

haver [pronounced to rhyme with SHAVER] talk nonsense; dither

what's he havering aboot? what's he drivelling on about?

head → **you'll have your head in your hands to play with** you'll be in trouble

heather → **it won't exactly set the heather alight** it won't cause much of a sensation; a phrase about as much used as the English equivalent: *it won't exactly set the Thames on fire.*

heavy This type of beer is the closest thing to English bitter.

heedrum hodrum A mocking term used by Scots to describe traditional Scottish music, the sort of music of which they are not fans; the word is also used to refer to the Gaelic language or (in the plural) to Gaelic speakers.

hee-haw a euphemistic expression emphasizing the negative: 1) not at all, absolutely not 2) nothing
ye can sing hee-haw you can't sing at all

heelie the crust or end piece of a loaf

heenies awa NORTH EAST a long time ago; a long way away

hegri SHETLAND heron

heid [pronounced HEED] head

heid-banger SLANG nutter, crazy person

heid-nip → SLANG **it's a real heid-nip** it really does my head in; I can't stand it

Heilandman's umbrella At Glasgow's Central Station, the railway bridge as it spans Argyll Street.

Heilander Highlander

hell → **hell mend her!** to hell with her!

hems → **to put the hems on** to ruin, to put an end to, to do away with

hen Used in the Glasgow area as a form of address to a woman, either an acquaintance or a stranger, this is the female equivalent of **Jimmy**.

is that your bag ye left there, hen?

hers → **we went back to hers** we went back to her place

het In a children's game of tag or tig **het** is the kid who has been caught and who now has to chase the others. (Normally called *it* in Southern English).

het NORTH EAST hot

heuch NORTH EAST 1) cliff 2) ravine

heuchter-teuchter A word used in a mocking and derogatory way by Scots to refer to the sort of stereotypically Scottish things they don't think much of, like **heuchter-teuchter music** or **heuchter-teuchter dancing**.

High Court of Justiciary LEGAL SCOTS the supreme criminal court

high doh go to **doh**

high heid yin [pronounced high-HEED-yun] 1) boss 2) important person, VIP

Higher This is an examination which is taken at the end of the fifth or sixth year at a Scottish school at the age of 16 or 17. Although the exam is taken at an earlier age than English A levels, Scottish kids normally take a wider range of Highers than English kids do at A level.

Highland Games Highland games are spectacles that combine music and sport. You'll get tossing the caber, highland dancing, pipe bands, beer tents etc. They can be traced back to the days when clan chiefs would audition to find the strongest warriors and best entertainers for their court.

Highland line an imaginary line dividing the Highlands of Scotland from the Lowlands and running from the Moray Firth to somewhere along the Clyde Estuary

hine NORTH EAST far

hine awa far away

he bides hine roon the corner he lives a long way away (North East Scots has an opposite of 'just round the corner') **hine doon the road** right down the road

hing GLASGOW thing

> **they're daein this karaoke hing the noo arra pub**

hingen NORTH EAST SLANG disgusting

hingy SLANG [pronounced to rhyme with CLINGY] unwell, under the weather

hinna NORTH EAST haven't

hirays, hireys EAST COAST SLANG money

hirple SHETLAND NORTH EAST limp; hobble

his → **we went back to his** we went back to his place

hiv NORTH EAST have

hoa(t)ch → **to hoach with something** to crawl with something, to be swarming with something

hoa(t)ching swarming, very busy

Hogmanay This is the Scottish New Year which is, some would say, more of a festival than Christmas. New Year celebrations held throughout Scotland include huge street parties in Edinburgh and Glasgow as well as **ceilidhs** and fireworks.

holm IN PLACE NAMES from the Old Norse ***holmr*** meaning *little island.* So **Lamb Holm** (a small island in Orkney).

holograph LEGAL SCOTS A legal document is **holograph** if entirely written in the writer's own handwriting. It does not require a witness' signature.

Holyrood (Palace) Holyrood Palace, at the foot of the **Royal Mile** in Edinburgh, was formerly the principal residence of the Scottish monarchs, and is now the official residence of the British monarch in Scotland. It was founded as an abbey in the 12th century, extended as a palace under James IV, and attained its present appearance in the early 1680s under Charles II.

Holyrood (Parliament) In 1999 the Scottish parliament was re-established after a lapse of 292 years. The new parliament building at the foot of the **Royal Mile**, a source of great controversy because of the extent to which it exceeded its original budget and timescale for completion, opened in October 2004. Certain matters (such as defence and economic policy) have been reserved to the UK parliament in Westminster.

homer If someone offers to do a job for you as a **homer**, then he'll be doing it in his own time, not his company's, and will expect cash for the work done.

Honours of Scotland This is the alternative name for the Scottish Crown Jewels (consisting of the crown, sceptre and sword of state) which are on display in the Crown Room of Edinburgh Castle along with the **Stone of Destiny**.

hoodie 1) a short jacket which has a hood to come up over the head 2) someone wearing one of these 3) a hooded crow

hoof → **to pad the hoof** to walk, to hoof it

hoojigapiv NORTH EAST OLDER SCOTS thingummyjig, whatsit

hoolet OLDER SCOTS an owl

hoose house

hornie EAST COAST SLANG policeman

the hornies the police

horse into NORTH EAST To **horse into** food is to get stuck into it with enthusiasm.

host SHETLAND cough

houghmagandie sexual cavorting, a humorous or calvinistically humorless term

how

> In Scotland this can, confusingly for others, also mean *why*.
> **I don't love you any more – how?**
> baffling to the English ear
> **I stopped him going out – how?**
> confusion here; is it the means or the reason that's being asked about?; context will normally decide

howe IN PLACE NAMES from the Old Norse ***haug-r*** meaning a *mound*. So **Howe of the Mearns**: moor hill.

howf(f) OLDER SCOTS A shelter or meeting place, this older word is still found in pub names like Burns' Howff. The hut on a building site might also be known as a **howff**.

howk dig

huddery scruffy

hudgie a ride taken by hanging on the back of a van etc

ah'll gie ye a hudgie on ma bike

huff → **in the huff** English would be: in a huff

hunner NORTH EAST hundred

hurdies NORTH EAST bottom, hips

you'll get a breeze up your hurdies wearing a kilt!

hurl a lift in a car; a car ride

ah'll gie ye a hurl doon the road, hen

hytering and skytering NORTH EAST stumbling, though the Scots paints a livelier picture of limbs flying about in all directions in an attempt not to hit the deck.

I

Ibrox the home of Glasgow Rangers

icicle NORTH EAST This can also mean an *ice lolly.*

idjit idiot

-ie This suffix is very widespread in Scots, particularly in the North East. As with its continental counterparts (like -chen, -lein, in German, -(t)je in Dutch) it connotes not merely smallness, but expresses an affectionate attitude on the part of the speaker. Some examples: **mannie**; **wifie**; **laddie**; **gadgie**.

ilk → **of that ilk** If you happen to meet someone called, say, **Alan Dunmuir of that ilk**, then you have met someone who comes from a place called Dunmuir and who is also the **laird** or owner of that place.

ilka, ilky NORTH EAST OLDER SCOTS each; every

inaneth NORTH EAST OLDER SCOTS under

inby OLDER SCOTS inside (*a building*)

inch IN PLACE NAMES from the Gaelic ***innis*** meaning *island*. So **Inchcolm**: St Columba's Isle.

intae NORTH EAST This is sometimes used in place of *in*.
noo living intae anither place now living in another place
nae lowdy intae his pooch no money in his pocket

interdict LEGAL SCOTS injunction, banning order

intimations You may see this as a heading in a newspaper. The English equivalent would be *Births, Marriages and Deaths*.

inver IN PLACE NAMES from the Gaelic ***inbhir*** meaning *river mouth*. So **Inverness**: Nessmouth.

Iona Abbey In 563 AD St Columba founded a Celtic monastery on this little island off the west coast of Scotland. Through the centuries Iona became a place of pilgrimage and a burial place for kings (Scottish, Norwegian and Irish). In the middle ages a Benedictine abbey and a nunnery were built here. The abbey was restored early last century and this peaceful little island still attracts visitors from all over the world.

is

1) In Scots the verb form **is** can be used with plural subjects, apart from the personal subjects *we, you* and *they.*
the new glasses is all broken

2) In the North East you'll hear **is it** used as an equivalent of *isn't it.*
it's a fine day, is it?

-it In Scots this ending corresponds to -ed.

that's the fuel pump sortit

ither other

J

J can also be pronounced JAI to rhyme with SPY or HIGH, but only when saying the alphabet or spelling a word.

jack n jills RHYMING SLANG pills

Jacobites The name deriving from the Latin for James (*Jacobus*) was given to the supporters of James VII (and subsequently James Francis Edward Stewart and Bonnie Prince Charlie) who wanted to see the Stewart monarchy restored to the throne. Several uprisings took place between 1689 and 1746 with varying degrees of success. Final defeat came at the battle of **Culloden**. Subsequent measures ensured that no future Jacobite rebellions would occur and dramatically reduced the power of the **clan system**.

jag injection

Jags a nickname for Partick Thistle Football Club

jaikit jacket

jalouse NORTH EAST conclude; guess, suppose

Jambos a nickname for Heart of Midlothian football team, Hearts

jammy piece a jam sandwich

jannie janitor

jap splash

jeely 1) NORTH EAST jelly 2) jam

jeely piece a jam sandwich

jeezo! SLANG a fairly mild exclamation, like *heavens* or *crikey*

jessie SLANG an effeminate man (also used in the North of England)

jiggered exhausted, knackered

Jimmy GLASGOW A form of address for any man. This is often shortened to **Jim**. Unlike its female counterpart, **hen**, the word would not normally be used between two men who know each other.
gonnae move yer van there, Jim? can you move your van, mate

jiner joiner

jingbang → **the whole jingbang** the whole lot, the whole caboodle

jings! good heavens!

jist just

Jock Tamson's bairns → **we're a' Jock Tamson's bairns** we're all on this planet together and none of us is inherently any more or less deserving than another, we're all God's little children

Joe Baxi RHYMING SLANG taxi

jook same as **jukes**

josser → **auld josser** old bloke

jotter At school a **jotter** is an exercise book.
if she carries on like that, she'll be getting her jotters she'll get the sack

jouk dodge

jukes To put or hide something **up your jukes** means to put or hide it up the front of your clothing.

jungle → GLASGOW **The Jungle** is a nickname for the Celtic end at Celtic's home ground, Parkhead.

K

kaim NORTH EAST OLDER SCOTS comb

keech excrement, crap

keek look, peek

> **keek!** Scots wifies say **keek** to wee babies, while English ones go *peekaboo!*

keeker black eye

keelie the stereotypical Glaswegian, tough and defiant and working class

keepie-uppie A game or exercise involving one person and a football – you have to keep the ball in the air with little kicks, taps, headers, bounces off the knee etc.

keks SLANG underpants

Kelvinside A posh part of Glasgow, seen as posh particularly because of the (supposed) accent of its inhabitants; this is where *sex* refers to things you keep potatoes in, or where a *crèche* is an accident between two motor vehicles. Parallel to **Morningside** in Edinburgh.

ken EAST COAST know
dinna ken don't know

This is also used as a filler word.
I cannae face seeing her again, ken? ...know what I mean?
it'll be round here somewhere, ken it'll be round here somewhere, right

kenspeckle distinctive; prominent; well-known

kent known

kil IN PLACE NAMES from the Gaelic ***cill*** meaning *church*. So **Kilmarnock**: church of St Marnoc.

Killie a nickname for Kilmarnock football team

kilt If a Scot is going to wear a kilt (and not all do) then it is most likely to be for a special occasion like a wedding, a graduation ceremony or maybe an international rugby match.

kin[1] can

kin[2] IN PLACE NAMES from the Gaelic ***ceann*** meaning *head*. So **Kingussie**: head of the pinewood; **Kinlochleven**: head of Loch Leven.

kine cows, cattle

kinna kind of

kirk church

come into the body of the kirk come and join the main group; come and join us (*there is no religious connotation to this idiom*)

kirn 1) churn 2) NORTH EAST In the North East this can also be used to mean a *mess*

kist NORTH EAST OLDER SCOTS chest, storage box

kitchie deem NORTH EAST kitchen girl

kite SLANG same as **kyte**

klype tell tales. Also a noun.

the wee klype has telt the teacher

knacked 1) broken 2) done in; knackered

knock IN PLACE NAMES from the Gaelic ***cnoc*** meaning *hill*. So **Knockbain**: white hill.

knock back refuse, reject

knot → **she was fair knotting herself** she

was laughing her head off

knowe IN PLACE NAMES from the Old Norse ***knoll-r*** meaning *hilltop*.

knype on NORTH EAST [pronounced NIP] hurry up

kye cattle

kyle IN PLACE NAMES from the Gaelic ***caol*** meaning *strait*.

kypie NORTH EAST head

kyte SLANG belly
up the kyte pregnant

kythe OLDER SCOTS appear

L

labdick SLANG policeman

laekit → SHETLAND **weel laekit** well liked

laich IN PLACE NAMES lower; survives in names such **The Laich Hall** (*of a castle*). In lowland Scots a ***laich*** is a stretch of low-lying ground. The **Lake of Menteith** was originally the Laich of Menteith.

laird landowner; similar to a lord of the manor

laldy

A range of related uses.
to get laldy to get into trouble, to get a telling off
he'll be getting laldy when he gets

home
give it laldy really go for it
in the second half of the gig the band really gave it laldy
the couple in the hotel room next door were giving it laldy
he gave him laldy he gave him a good beating

Lallans Another name for Lowland Scots, the word is also used to describe a largely artificial variety of Scots concocted by the poet Hugh McDiarmid, a language that has great force of expression, but is no real mirror of spoken linguistic reality.

lam → **have a lam on** SLANG be annoyed, be pissed off

lane alone
I cudnae gae ma lane I couldn't go alone

lang long

langsome NORTH EAST OLDER SCOTS boring

larick NORTH EAST OLDER SCOTS larch

lave NORTH EAST OLDER SCOTS rest, remainder

laverock NORTH EAST OLDER SCOTS lark (*the feathered type*)

leader-aff GLASGOW gang leader

learin NORTH EAST education

leck IN PLACE NAMES from the Gaelic ***leac***

meaning *flat stone* or a *slope of flat stones*. So **Lechkine**: place of flat stones; **Auchinleck**: field of the flat stones.

lee NORTH EAST a lie

Lee Marvin RHYMING SLANG starving

leet list

len NORTH EAST loan

tak a len of someone to take advantage of someone

lether NORTH EAST ladder

licensed grocer It's not that there are both official, respectable grocers and illegally operating bootleg grocers in Scotland, but that a licensed grocer is able to sell alcohol.

lift OLDER SCOTS sky

like

There are some distinctly Scots uses.

1) **like aat** SLANG like that. This is the Scots variant of a modern innovation used when relating events, either to introduce what somebody said or as reaction to something that was said or that happened. In the latter case it is followed by an unmistakable facial expression, from which the listener will appreciate the emotion of the speaker.

so he says, is that yur friend or yur ma yuh've brought wi yuh? n ah wuz like aat → cheeky wee bugger, so yuh are

he asks me up to his place, ah wuz like aat (*facial expression to match*)

2) **the likes of...** In English this normally has a negative connotation. Not so in Scots.

the likes of Douglas would have no problem stopping a shot at goal like that

3) **what like's the food?** a common Scots inversion. English would say: what's the food like?

4) **what'm I like!** silly me!

what's he like, eh? isn't he a character, eh?; can be said either in amusement or frustration

5) **likes, likesay** a filler, used to make a pause in a stream of speech; similar in use to *you know*

links[1] sausages

links[2] NORTH EAST the area of sand dunes going down to the shore

linn IN PLACE NAMES from Gaelic ***linn*** meaning *pool*. So **Linn of Dee**: pool of the River Dee.

lippen trust, rely on

loan lane

loch is a Gaelic word meaning *lake*

lochan small loch

Loch Lomond Not quite Scotland's longest loch (at 22.6 miles or 36.2km it's slightly shorter than Lochs Awe and Ness) but it is the largest expanse of water in Britain.

loon NORTH EAST boy

loons SLANG trousers

Lord Advocate LEGAL SCOTS the senior law officer in Scotland

Lord Provost In Glasgow, Edinburgh, Aberdeen and Dundee the **Lord Provost** is the mayor.

loun NORTH EAST boy

loup NORTH EAST jump

loupin 1) painful
ma heid's loupin my head's killing me
2) disgusting, revolting
the lager's loupin the lager's disgusting
3) crawling, infested
the city centre's loupin with tourists

lowdy NORTH EAST money

loweing glowing

lowp same as **loup**

lum chimney
lang may yer lum reek literally: long may your chimney smoke, so: good luck to you, have a long and successful life

lumber SLANG pick-up
get a lumber pick up a girl (or a boy)
oot looking furra lumber

M

ma my

maalie SHETLAND
fulmar

Mac..., Mc...
The common prefix in Scots surnames is from the Gaelic meaning *son of.*

machair low, grassy land at the back of beaches, particularly on the Western Isles

maddy crazy person, can be an affectionate term

maet SHETLAND food

mair more

mairrit married

maist most

mak make

makar a Scots poet laureate

malky razor (*as a weapon*)

man

> **my man** This would sound absurdly antiquated or class-ridden if spoken with an English (southern) accent; but in the Glasgow area (spoken: ma man) it's pally.

mannie NORTH EAST just means *man*

> **we waited at the garage for the mannie to find the loo keys**

manse vicarage

manto EAST COAST SLANG chicks, women
the manto's hoachin there are chicks everywhere

mantovani RHYMING SLANG (= *fanny*) chicks, women, totty

Marches → Riding the Marches
A ceremony in Borders towns when

horsemen patrol the boundaries of common land (known as **marches**).

maroc SLANG drunk

mart day NORTH EAST market day

masel myself

maucht NORTH EAST OLDER SCOTS effort, attempt

maun must

mavis a thrush (*a rather literary word*)

maw mother

mebbe maybe

meen NORTH EAST moon

merry dancers SHETLAND the Northern Lights, the Aurora Borealis

messages also: shopping, usually groceries

> **I had that many messages I decided to get a taxi**

mibbe maybe

michty (me)! NORTH EAST good heavens!

mickle → **mony a mickle maks a muckle** might be said, for example, to someone who contributes a small amount to a collection; lots of little bits can add up to something big

midden This is the place where dustbins are kept, usually around the back of a **tenement** block. It can also be a *rubbish* *tip* or, out in the country, a *dung heap*. There are of course extended uses:

seen their office?, what a midden!

midder SHETLAND mother

midge A midge is a small biting flying insect, particularly common in the north and west of Scotland over the summer months (but it is making its way progressively further south). They hover around in inescapable swarms and will get up your nose, in your ears, down your collar, into your mouth. Unlike holiday-makers, midges don't like hot sunshine. So when the sun's out, you'll be safe. But in the evening, or in the drizzle, or in the early morning, when you're loading up the car, out they come. Their main human characteristic is that they are supposed to find a strong reek of garlic repellent.

midgie 1) same as **midge** 2) same as **midden**

midgie man a refuse collector, not to be confused with the following

midgie raker a down-and-out who scavenges in dustbins and litterbins

min NORTH EAST man; a way of addressing any male, like **mon** in older Scots.

aricht min! alright chum!

mince SLANG rubbish
he's talking a loada mince
see these new cartons, pure mince these new cartons are rubbish
yer heid's mince you're just not with it

mind also: remember
do you mind when we...? do you remember when we...?

minder, mindin a small gift; a souvenir; a New Year's present

mine → **at mine** at my place

mines mine

> All the other personal pronouns add an s to the possessive adjective (your/yours; our/ours etc) and Scots does the same for *mine*.

minister Scottish churches have ministers rather than vicars.

mink NORTH EAST a dirty individual, a social outcast

mintee, mintie NORTH EAST minute
wait a mintie wait a minute

mintit SLANG great, brilliant

mirackle SHETLAND injure severely

miroclous GLASGOW drunk (a contortion of miraculous)

mirry dancers SHETLAND the Northern

Lights, the Aurora Borealis

misanter SHETLAND accident

mischanter NORTH EAST accident (The c is not pronounced).

miss yourself miss out on a good time

> **och, ye should've been there, great party, ye really missed yerself**

missives LEGAL SCOTS If you are buying or selling a house then the missives are all the legal documents that are drawn up relating to the sale. When ***missives are concluded*** then the sale is complete.

mither OLDER SCOTS mother

mixter-maxter mish-mash; a bit of this and a bit of that

mo'uh SLANG This book is not attempting to put all the re-articulations of accent into print. But this one is so common. If you're a traveller in Scotland, you should know that your **mo'uh**, especially if you're driving around the Glasgow area, is your car (it's also Cockney, of course).

mochie NORTH EAST wet, dreary and dismal

mochit NORTH EAST filthy

Mod Festival of Gaelic music held in October including singing, dancing and piping competitions. The location changes every year.

Moderator In the Church of Scotland the Moderator is the person elected to chair meetings of Church Assemblies.

modren NORTH EAST modern

mon NORTH EAST man; usually as an interjection

> **ye'll no find him at hame the day, mon**

Mons Meg a 6 ton medieval siege gun now housed in Edinburgh Castle

mony many

moocher → NORTH EAST **he's a moocher** he's always borrowing things

moorit SHETLAND light brown (the colour of Shetland sheep)

moosey-faced miserable-looking

moothie a mouthorgan

more IN PLACE NAMES from the Gaelic ***mòr*** meaning *big*. So **Aviemore**: big hill face.

morn → **the morn** tomorrow
the morn's morn tomorrow morning

Morningside A posh part of Edinburgh; the word has connotations of gentility and a Morningside accent definitely sets you aside from the hoi-polloi, this being the place where people think that *sex* is what people in olden days used to buy coal in. Similar to **Kelvinside** in Glasgow.

morra → GLASGOW **the morra** tomorrow

mouth music A technique comparable to scat in jazz or rapping without actual words, **mouth music** is nonsense words sung in imitation of the sound of the bagpipes. It originated in 1745 when playing the bagpipes was prohibited.

mowrie NORTH EAST sandy shingle

mowrie beach NORTH EAST shingly beach

mowser moustache

MSP member of the Scottish parliament

muckle big; much
nae muckle luck not much luck

mull a peninsula or headland

Munro any Scottish mountain over 3,000 feet (914m)

Munro-bagging climbing Scottish mountains over 3,000 feet as a kind of collector's hobby

Murrayfield the home of Scottish international rugby

N

na IN PLACE NAMES Gaelic for *of*

nae no; not

nash EAST COAST SLANG hurry
goat tae nash gotta go, gotta dash

naw no

neb SLANG nose
to take a neb at something to take a look at something

ned yob, yobbo
the neds keep smashing the glass at the bus stop

neddy yobbish
me in a white shellsuit? ah'd just look pure neddy, so ah would

nedette a female ned

need

Two distinctly Scots constructions with this verb:

1) **it needs painted/specified**

The use of the past participle is normal Scots here. Non-Scots would use the present participle and say *it needs painting/specifying*

2) a fairly complex construction:
you wouldnae need tae be saving yer money it's a good job you're not

trying to save money, it's just as well you're not trying to save money

neen NORTH EAST none

ne'erday New Year's Day

neesik SHETLAND porpoise

neist next

ness SHETLAND headland

Nessie This is the name given to the Loch Ness Monster; there's only one name though for all the sightings; you'd have thought that if the loch actually has had a monster in it all this time, there must be at least two of them just so as to keep the monster family going...

neuk corner; nook

news NORTH EAST chat

he drapped in for a news he dropped in for a chat

to have a bit of a news to have a chat

nicht night

the nicht tonight

nickum NORTH EAST a rascal, a mischief-maker

nip hurt

it's still nippin a wee bit, but I'll survive

to nip someone's heid to annoy

someone by nagging

nippie NORTH EAST an informal word for a waitress

nippie sweetie GLASGOW a sharp-tongued person

nippit tight, tight-fitting

nithing NORTH EAST nothing

no also means **not**

> **will ye no stop for a wee drink?**
> **it's getting a wee bit late, is it no?**

nocht OLDER SCOTS nothing

nondy SLANG stupid

noo → **the noo** (right) now

> This also has the dual usage of English *just now* or *right now* referring both to the present and to a time just past.
> **he was sitting right there the noo**

noost SHETLAND a hollow on the shore where a boat is kept

nor In Scots this can also have the meaning of *than*.
mair nor that more than that

not

> **you've heard him sing, have you not?**
>
> To southern English ears this is a very formal sounding construction

and would be replaced in speech by *haven't you*. There is nothing formal about the Scots usage.

notion → to take a notion to someone to take a liking to someone; to fancy someone

numpty SLANG silly person

nyaff 1) small or insignificant person 2) irritating, stupid, unimportant person

when the boss puts his old raincoat on he looks jist like a wee nyaff
get aff the sofa and dae some decoratin, ye useless great nyaff!

O

ocht anything

offski SLANG leaving, going, off

11 o'clock, time I was offski

Old Firm game a football match between Celtic and Rangers

ony [pronounced to rhyme with TONY] any

oo SHETLAND wool

oor our

oosey fluffy, with bits of fluff coming off

ma new sweater's gone all oosey

oot out

ootay out of

or (eest) NORTH EAST until

> **ah'm waitressing the noo or (eest) ah find somethin better**

orra[1] coarse

orra[2] GLASGOW all the

orraman odd-job man

ory dirty

outsider In Glasgow this is more than just a sociological concept: it is also the crust of a loaf of bread.

outwith outside; outside of; beyond
outwith the scope of this agreement

ower over
ah'm no ower auld tae... I'm not too old to...

owre over

oxter armpit

P

P&J (=Press and Journal) a daily newspaper for the whole of northern Scotland

P3, P4 etc primary 3, primary 4 etc in school

pairk, park also means a *field*

pal

> One of the most commonly used terms to address another person. But it's not always that friendly, as the tone of voice will let you know.
> **goat a light, pal?**
> **that's no very nice, pal, you need tae watch yer step**

pan loaf → NORTH EAST **to put on the pan loaf** to try to speak with a posh accent

pan → SLANG **to knock your pan in** to knacker or exhaust yourself

panel[1] LEGAL SCOTS If a lawyer in a courtroom refers to the **panel**, then he is referring to the accused standing in the dock.

panel[2] SLANG hit, clout

Paradise Celtic Park

Parkhead the home ground of Celtic football club

partan crab

paw father

pay-poke pay packet

pech NORTH EAST struggle; puff
she came peching her way into...
she came puffing and panting into...
what a pech it was to get up that hill

peedie In the Orkneys this means *little*.

peel a Borders fortified tower

peely-wally pale and unhealthy looking

> **the sunbed parlour lures the peely-wally**
> **the whole decor's a tad too peely-wally for my taste**

peenge NORTH EAST OLDER SCOTS whinge

peer NORTH EAST poor

peerie[1] SHETLAND little

peerie[2] top, spinning top

pend arch; archway

perr poor

photie photo

pibroch a piece of music for the bagpipes consisting of a theme plus elaborate variations on the theme

Picts The first inhabitants of what was to become Scotland have left traces of their lives in the form of standing stones all over the country but particularly in the North East. Very little is known about these mysterious people, first referred to by a Roman writer in 297 AD, who seem to have disappeared by the middle of the 9th century, possibly overrun by the Scots, who moved across from the west.

piece also: 1) sandwich 2) slice of bread

pinkie the little finger (also used in northern parts of England and in the USA)

pints NORTH EAST [pronounced to rhyme with HINTS] shoelaces

pish SLANG piss

pished SLANG pissed, drunk

pit put

Pittodrie Aberdeen's football stadium

plank NORTH EAST hide; hide away

plantie-crub SHETLAND small round stone enclosure for growing cabbages

plat In the language of builders and architects this is a platform or a flat piece of stone or cement.

play If a person is said to be **playing**

himself/herself this simply means that he/she is playing or having fun or playing around.

playpiece This is a snack for a schoolkid to eat at playtime, usually a biscuit or packet of crisps.

pled This is the standard Scots past simple of the verb *to plead.*

plenishin OLDER SCOTS furniture

plook zit, pimple

plooky covered with pimples

plooky or no, ah'm gonna snog him

plouk same as **plook**

plowter about splash about, flounder about (*in water, in snow*)

poind LEGAL SCOTS [pronounced PIND to rhyme with SINNED] seize or impound (*goods for the payment of debt*)

poinding LEGAL SCOTS [pronounced PINDING] the seizure of goods for the payment of debt

poke (little) bag
a poke of chips a bag of chips
wi aw his worldly goods in an auld plastic poke

pokey hat ice-cream cone

policies LEGAL SCOTS The **policies** of a property are the grounds round about it.

polis [the stress is reversed to give the pronunciation POH-lis] 1) police 2) policeman

pooch NORTH EAST pocket

postie postman; postwoman

pouffe In Scotland this piece of furniture is pronounced [pooFAY] not [poof]. Wonder why.

pree NORTH EAST OLDER SCOTS taste, sample

press a shallow cupboard set into a wall

Prestonpans (Battle of) This battle in September 1745 just to the east of Edinburgh saw the **Jacobites** under Bonnie Prince Charlie defeat the Hanoverian forces led by Sir John Cope. The result was significant not only because it constituted a psychological boost to the Jacobite cause but also because it meant that a large proportion of Scotland was now under Jacobite control.

principal teacher head of department

procurator fiscal LEGAL SCOTS public prosecutor

provost mayor

puckle → **a puckle** a little; a few; several

puddock frog

puff → SLANG **in my puff** in my life

on yer puff on your own

puirtith NORTH EAST OLDER SCOTS poverty

pure GLASGOW

A common, especially Glaswegian, slang intensifier.

ah pure wish ah could I really wish I could

pure dead brilliant absolutely, totally brilliant

his oxters were pure mingin his armpits stank like nobody's business

pursuer LEGAL SCOTS plaintiff

pus SLANG face

Q

quaich a shallow, two-handled drinking vessel

quean, quine, quinie NORTH EAST girl

R

ra

In Glaswegian speech the word *the* often turns into **ra** and merges with surrounding words.

werra keys? where are the keys?

ye gonna gerra bus? are you going to get the bus?

gorra cash? got the cash?

radge EAST COAST SLANG crazy bastard; bastard
Also an adjective and adverb: crazy, wild
seen the radge paintings the guy does?
going radge on the terraces going wild on the terraces

raffle → **away ye go and raffle yourself** get knotted, get lost, don't bother me

raivelt NORTH EAST OLDER SCOTS confused

rammy fight, brawl

randan → **to go out on the randan** to go out to have a good time, round the pubs, clubs etc

rare This can also mean *great* or *brilliant*.
and a right rare time was had by all and we all had a great old time

rasp raspberry

rax NORTH EAST reach

redd up SHETLAND tidy

reef NORTH EAST roof

reek smoke

reestit mutton SHETLAND smoke-dried mutton

reiver raider, robber in the Scottish Borders in former times

rerr rare; great, tremendous

reset LEGAL SCOTS receive and sell on (*stolen goods*), fence (*stolen goods*)

rhone 1) gutter (*on the roof*) 2) short for **rhonepipe**

rhonepipe drainpipe

rickle → **she was just a rickle of banes** she was just a bag of bones, she was all skin and bones
a rickle of stones a heap of stones

right → **that'll be right!** a sarcastic way of disagreeing or saying *no, I don't think so*

> **me lend you £55? aye, that'll be right**

rikkin lum NORTH EAST a smoking chimney, therefore an inhabited house

rin NORTH EAST run

rock n roll → RHYMING SLANG **on the rock n roll** on the dole

rocklum a chimney in a rockface

rone same as **rhone**

ronepipe same as **rhonepipe**

ros, ross IN PLACE NAMES from both the **Brittonic** and the Gaelic for promontory or wood. So **Kinross**: head of the cape.

roup LEGAL SCOTS auction

rousht NORTH EAST rust
stick wi me n yer tackits'll niver rousht I'll look after you (literally: stick with me and your hobnailed boots will never rust)

row [pronounced to rhyme with HOW]→

to give somebody a row to tell somebody off, to bawl somebody out

rowth NORTH EAST OLDER SCOTS a large number; a large amount
a fair rowth o money quite a lot of money

Royal Highland Show One of the UK's largest agricultural shows, held in June every year just outside Edinburgh. Highlights include displays of animals, food and drink exhibitions and competitions.

Royal Mile The street leading from Edinburgh Castle down to Holyrood Palace. Going down from the castle, it's made up of Castlehill, Lawnmarket, High Street, Canongate and Abbey Strand.

S

S1, S2 etc the first and second year etc in a secondary school

saa SHETLAND 1) saw 2) so

sae so

saft soft

sair 1) sore, painful 2) hard, difficult
A North East Scots idiom: **it's a sair fecht** life's a struggle; things are difficult

sair erse NORTH EAST SLANG moaner

sannie 1) sandwich 2) sandals, sandshoes

sark OLDER SCOTS shirt

sarking the boards or felt directly beneath the slates or tiles of a roof

sasine LEGAL SCOTS To give **sasine** to someone is to transfer legal ownership of feudal property to that person.

Sasines → LEGAL SCOTS **Register of Sasines** the land registry, that records details of property ownership and transfers

Sassenach 1) Englishman; Englishwoman 2) English

sauchie from the Lowland Scots for *a place full of willows.* So **Sauchiehall Street**, Glasgow (**Sauchie Haugh**: low-lying ground covered with willow trees)

-say a common ending; but the actual derivation is the Norse word *ey* meaning island. So **Whalsay:** whale island.

scaffie NORTH EAST binman

scants pants, underpants

scarf SHETLAND shag (*the feathered type*)

scart NORTH EAST scratch

scattald SHETLAND common grazing land

schemie a person who lives on a housing estate

schochle NORTH EAST shuffle

sclater NORTH EAST slater

sclim OLDER SCOTS to climb

scoobied SLANG clueless, useless

scoocher NORTH EAST beggar

scoosh SLANG do easily
ah'll scoosh it it'll be a doddle
ah scooshed the exam the exam was dead easy

scoosh case → SLANG
the exam was a scoosh case the exam was dead easy

Scotch pie go to the **Menu Reader**

Scots, Scottish, Scotch

As an adjective **Scots** is normally used in connection with things linguistic, so you might talk about
a Scots word

or
an old Scots usage.

The Scots themselves find it irksome if someone says
he is Scots.

It is preferable to say
he is Scottish

or
he is a Scot.

The most generally used adjective is **Scottish**. You can't really go wrong with this one.

The word **Scotch** is likely, if misused, to put backs up in Scotland. Basically **Scotch** is restricted to a smallish number of set collocations, for example

Scotch broth, Scotch egg, Scotch mist, Scotch pie, Scotch whisky.

Never say of someone that

he/she is Scotch!

scour about NORTH EAST look around

scrambled eggs RHYMING SLANG legs

scran SLANG food

scratcher SLANG bed

ah'll bide in ma scratcher till lunchtime I'm going to stay in bed until lunchtime

scregh screech, scream

the scregh of the wind

screive OLDER SCOTS scribble

scunner disgust, put off

I've scunnert masel wi... I've had so much... that I'm sick of it

would that no scunner ye! that really is the limit!

The word is also used as a noun.

there's the old scunner there's the

old so-and-so
the scunners! the sods!

scunnering disgusting; irritating

scunnert disgusted; pissed off; fed up

scutter aboot NORTH EAST 1) mess about 2) chase about
Also used as a noun.
getting everything ready for the party was a fair scutter aboot it was some hassle getting everything ready

sea-loch a loch that is open to the sea

see

1) The word **see** can be used to point up the subject of a sentence, to make sure the listener realizes just who you are talking about before you say what you want to say about that person (which might well be yourself).
see ma wife, she's no too pleased aboot this
she hates it, but see me, ah love it
see tapas, magic tapas are absolutely fantastic.

Note the amazing concision of the Scots here.

2) **See** in Scots can also be used to mean *to give*.
see's a go on yer bike give us a go on your bike

see's back ma jaikit give me my jacket back

seek → he's never had his worries to seek he has always had quite enough worries

selkie SHETLAND seal

Selkie can also mean a mythical creature which sometimes takes the form of a seal and sometimes a person.

selt sold

sen since

sgian-dubh same as **skean dhu**

shalder SHETLAND oyster catcher

sharn NORTH EAST OLDER SCOTS dung

sheltie a Shetland pony

sheriff LEGAL SCOTS equivalent to a JP in England

Sheriff Court LEGAL SCOTS Most Scottish towns will have a **Sheriff Court**, where a wide range of criminal and civil cases are heard. The High Court is reserved for trials of the most serious criminal offences.

Sheriff's officer LEGAL SCOTS His duties include raising legal actions on instruction by a lawyer, collecting debts and delivering summonses.

Sherman Tank RHYMING SLANG Yank, American

sherrikin telling off

shiel(in) OLDER SCOTS shelter; hut

shilpet SHETLAND sour

shilpit skinny, starved-looking

shining bright → RHYMING SLANG **that'll be shining bright** a humorous version of the ironic **that'll be right**, ie no, not likely, who do you think you're kidding

> **£120 for a pair a they jeans, aye that'll be shining bright**

shinty Shinty is a fast-moving game played by two teams of 14 players each on a pitch that can be up to 145 metres by 90 metres. Both sides of the stick, known as a **caman** or **hurley**, can be used to strike the ball. The ball can be hit above head height (unlike in hockey). And swinging the stick above head height is also allowed.

shoatie → **to keep shoatie** to keep lookout

shoogle shake, wobble

> **hey, dinna shoogle they cans aboot**

shoogly shaky, wobbly

shoon OLDER SCOTS shoes

shop → NORTH EAST **Dad's through the shop**

> In Aberdeen and the North East this means that *Dad is around the house somewhere* or that *Dad's in the next room* or that *Dad's in the next office.*

short leet shortlist

shottie → **to keep shottie** to keep lookout

show of presents a party held by a bride-to-be shortly before her wedding to show her friends the wedding presents she has been given

shtumer SLANG idiot

shuggle shake

shuggly shaky, wobbly

shunky SLANG toilet

sic such

sicht sight

sick line sick note, a note from a doctor confirming that a person is not fit for work

sidieways sideways

siller NORTH EAST OLDER SCOTS money

simmer dim SHETLAND the light night

around mid-summer

simmet NORTH EAST vest; shirt

single end a tenement flat with just one room; no toilet; not many left these days

single fish a piece of fish without the chips, when buying a **fish supper**

single malt a malt whisky that is distilled with the grain and water of one particular area only, as opposed to a **blended**

sitooterie a humorous invented word for a conservatory (the sort that people have built onto the back of their houses to maximize the enjoyment of sunshine, or grow plants in)

skaith NORTH EAST wound

Skara Brae A storm in Orkney in 1850 uncovered the best preserved prehistoric village in northern Europe. Various houses are clearly visible along with connecting passageways, stone furniture and artefacts.

skean dhu a Gaelic term [pronounced SKI-UN DOO] the traditional dagger (though it can barely open an envelope), carried stuffed down the side of a sock, when the kilt is worn

skeelie, skeely NORTH EAST OLDER SCOTS skilled

skelf splinter

skelly-eyed boss-eyed

skelp smack, hit
ye're no allowed tae skelp yer wean these days you're not allowed to smack your child these days

skelpin smacking, smack

skime gleam

skink go to the **Menu Reader**

skirlie NORTH EAST go to the **Menu Reader**

skite to slide; to slip
SLANG **oot onra skite** out getting boozed up

skitie slippery

skitter NORTH EAST 1) fiddly, time-consuming job 2) a very small amount
ah've nae a skitter tae ma name I've not a penny to my name

skitters → **the skitters** the runs, diarrhoea

skoosh 1) squirt 2) same as **scoosh**

skoosher a non-technical word for the windscreen washer on a car

skreich of day daybreak

sky rocket RHYMING SLANG pocket

slàinte a Gaelic word [pronounced SLANJ] meaning *cheers!, your health!*; if you want to use a fuller variant, try saying: **slàinte mhath** [pronounced SLANJ-JA VAH]. It means *good health.*

slaister NORTH EAST 1) spill, dribble
2) a person who eats in a messy manner

slater woodlouse

sleekit sly, cunning

sleep in oversleep

> **sorry I'm late boss, I slept in**
> In Scotland this is a possible excuse (unlike in England where it would be the equivalent of saying **sorry I'm late boss, I decided to have a lie-in.**)

slevvery wet, slimy

smeik smoke

smirr drizzle
a smirr of snow a light brushing of snow

smorrin NORTH EAST stuffed up
smorrin with the cold stuffed up with a cold

snaw bree NORTH EAST OLDER SCOTS slush (*snow*)

sneckit snarled up, caught

snib door catch
to leave the door on the snib to leave the door unlocked but shut with a catch so that it cannot be opened from the outside

so

> In combination with a verb this can

be used as a way of emphasizing what has been said.
he's right wee bastard, so he is

soapdodger SLANG a dirty, smelly individual

soapy bubble GLASGOW RHYMING SLANG trouble

couldnae keep ootay the soapy bubble

solan SHETLAND gannet

some → NORTH EAST **it was some much for them** it was too much for them

sonsy OLDER SCOTS beautiful, attractive in a plump and cheery sort of way

sook SLANG same as **souk**

soor sour

sotter NORTH EAST mess
fit a sotter! what a mess!

souk SLANG [pronounced SOOK] person who sucks up to people in authority

spaegie SHETLAND muscle ache after exertion

spaiver flies (*on trousers*)

speir [pronounced SPEAR] ask, enquire

speuggie sparrow

spite → **to have a spite against** to have it in for

split-new brand-new

spoot SHETLAND razor clam

sporran the large pouch, traditionally made of fur, that hangs from a man's belt in front of the kilt

spud NORTH EAST In the North East of Scotland if you have a **spud** in your tights, then you'll have a hole in them and not a potato.

spuds GLASGOW SLANG feet

spunk NORTH EAST a match (the kind you strike). But in the North East you wouldn't say *strike* – instead you **crack** a spunk.

spurtle a traditional porridge stirrer

square go a fight one to one

St Andrew's Day Scotland's patron saint is celebrated every year on 30 November with various events throughout the country.

St Kilda St Kilda is an archipelago off the west coast of Scotland, beyond the Outer Hebrides. The islands have been uninhabited since 1930 when the remaining population requested evacuation back to the mainland because of the extreme isolation. The islands are now a World Heritage Site and comprise Europe's most important seabird colony.

stance In Scotland taxis wait at a **stance** not a *rank*.

stane stone

stank drain; gutter

stapped → **the fridge is stapped** the fridge is stuffed full

stappit full stuffed full, crammed

stave sprain

he staved his ankle/finger

stay

In Scots **to stay** also means *to live*. This can be a source of some confusion for English people for whom the word **stay** has the connotation of something temporary. The following totally ridiculous conversation took place with a Glasgow taxi-driver.
taxi-driver: **been staying in Glasgow long?**
English passenger: **no, I live here**

steamboats SLANG drunk

steamie A public washhouse, for washing clothes. They no longer exist but are a part of modern Scottish history, featuring in plays and novels.

steamin SLANG drunk

steekit mist SHETLAND thick fog

stew NORTH EAST In the North East **stew** is also *dirt*.

stirk bullock

stoat SLANG hit
to stoat the baw to knock a ball about

> But this also has an extended meaning: to be a pedophile; to be a child molester

stoat-the-baw SLANG child abuse; cradle snatching

stoat down SLANG pour down

stoater SLANG 1) an especially attractive girl 2) something that is a very good example of its kind

> **yer mither wuz a wee stoater those days**
> **wan stoater of a dent you've got in your new motor there, eh?**

stock jacket the short jacket worn with the kilt

Stone of Destiny Also known as the **Stone of Scone**, this stone has been used as part of enthronement ceremonies since the 9th century for Scottish, English and British monarchs. In 1296 Edward I of

England removed the stone from Scone where it had been kept since Scone became the capital of the Scottish kingdom in around 840 AD and took it to Westminster Abbey. There it remained (except for a brief period of 4 months in 1950 when it was repossessed by Scottish nationalists and left outside Arbroath Abbey) until its symbolic return to Scotland on **St Andrew's Day** 1996. It can now be seen alongside the **Honours of Scotland** in the Crown Room of Edinburgh Castle.

Stone of Scone same as **Stone of Destiny**

Stonehaven fireball festival
Annual fire festival to welcome the New Year when locals swing large balls of burning material on the end of a wire in a procession through the town's streets.

stookie a plaster cast on a broken arm or leg

Also used as a slang verb meaning *to hit* (Scots has an amazing number of verbs for this action).
he stookied him and ran off with his mobile

stoon a small sharp pain

stoor 1) dust 2) a cloud of dust/smoke/steam etc

> In the North East if you burn something while cooking then a person coming into the room might say:
> **fit a stoor!**

stooshie same as **stushie**

stot bounce

> **the rain was fair stottin off the tent roof**

stotious SLANG drunk

stoup OLDER SCOTS jug, pitcher

stour same as **stoor**

stovies NORTH EAST go to the **Menu Reader**

stowed out packed, crowded

> **the bar was stowed out, nae chance of a seat**

stramash [pronounced with the stress on the last syllable] commotion; pushing and shoving

> **a right stramash in the goalmouth there was until the ball was finally booted clear**

strath from the Gaelic ***srath*** meaning *broad river plain.* So **Strathspey:** plain of the Spey; **Strathclyde:** plain of the Clyde.

strippit NORTH EAST OLDER SCOTS striped

stushie commotion, fuss, quarrel; fight

suit

> A Scot is more likely to say **you suit blue** than *blue suits you.*

supper

> If you go to a fish and chip shop you can have a **fish supper**, a **steak pie supper**, a **sausage supper** – these are served all day (not just at supper time) and will be chips plus fish/steak pie/sausage etc.

swaabie SHETLAND black-backed gull

swadgie SLANG look

gieza swadgie o yer mobile give us a look at your mobile

swallie a drink
ah had a swallie wi Murdo efter I had a couple of drinks with Murdo afterwards
a nice wee swallie a nice drink

swedge SLANG fight

swedgin SLANG fighting

sweetie wife an effeminate sort of man, especially an older one

swick NORTH EAST cheat
to swick the queue to jump the queue

swither be undecided; dither, hesitate

> **I'm swithering between going out or staying in**

sybie spring onion

syne OLDER SCOTS since; then; ago

T

T in the Park annual pop music festival held over a weekend in July near Kinross, Fife

tabbie NORTH EAST cigarette end, dog-end

tablet type of sweet, like fudge but usually harder

tacketties big boots

tackits NORTH EAST big boots

tae to; too

tail → **with the ticket in ma tail** with the

ticket in my pocket

tak take

tammy short for **Tam o'Shanter**, a man's round flat hat, no brim, with a bobble on top

tammy norie SHETLAND puffin

tang NORTH EAST seaweed

Tannadice the home stadium of Dundee United FC

tap 1) top
2) loan
he's always looking for a tap he's always trying to borrow some money

tappit tufted (*of a chicken*)

tapsalteerie OLDER SCOTS topsy-turvy

tattie-bogie, tattie bogle NORTH EAST scarecrow

tattie howkin NORTH EAST potato harvesting

tatties 1) potatoes 2) NORTH EAST SLANG finished, done for; dead; in big trouble; rubbish

that report is tatties that report is rubbish

tatties ower the side done for, beat

tawse a leather strap as used by teachers for punishing schoolchildren, a practice which has now been abolished

tay IN PLACE NAMES from the Gaelic ***taigh*** meaning *house*. So **Taynuilt**: house on the stream.

tea

In Scotland your **tea** is your supper, your main evening meal. The meal has generated some idioms.

your tea's oot you're in trouble

I knew if I did that ma tea was oot I knew if I did that I would be in trouble

your tea'll be up in a minute you're heading for trouble

you'll have had your tea Said to a visitor who drops in just around supper time by someone who doesn't really relish the idea of making a meal for this visitor, since that would be too much effort or even involve some expense. These days the expression is normally used in a tongue-in-cheek way.

tear → NORTH EAST **to give someone a tear of lip** to be very cheeky or rude to someone

teckit SHETLAND thatched

teen took

teip NORTH EAST SLANG [pronounced TYPE] condom

teip up NORTH EAST SLANG wear a condom; put on a condom

telt told

telt ye! told you so!

tenement block of flats built on several storeys around a single entrance passage, known as a **close**; in Scotland the word tenement is not a pejorative term

teuch NORTH EAST tough, as in describing a piece of meat

teuchter [pronounced CHUCHTER]
Highlander, though this has a slightly mocking overtone, so best not to call a Highlander a **teuchter** to his face (or to his friend's face).

thae those

that

Some typically Scots constructions, puzzling to the non-Scot:

is that you had your lunch? have you had your lunch?
is that you? have you finished?; are you ready?; is that all you want?
that's me lost I'm lost
that's no it finished it's not finished yet

that's the train just away the train has just left
you tell him that and that'll be you you'll be in trouble

Here's a bit of chat when collecting dry-cleaning:

have ye got the ticket?
(shop assistant takes ticket): **that's us then** = right, thanks
(shop assistant hands over dry-cleaning):
and that's you then = there you are

thegither together

they those

> This is often assumed by English-speakers to be an incorrect usage. The word, also written **thae**, is in fact an old Scots plural form of *that*, quite distinct in origin (but not in sound) from the personal pronoun *they*.
> **he's got wanny they DVD players** he's got one of those DVD players

thocht NORTH EAST thought

thole tolerate, stand; endure

thon NORTH EAST that (over there); those (over there). North Eastern Scots, has an extra word for *that* and *those* when the reference is more remote from the speaker.

thought → **it's a thought having to go back to work the next day** it's a daunting prospect...

thrang hectic

thrapple throat

thrawn awkward; argumentative; pig-headed

through → **to come through** can, in Central Scotland, mean either to come to Edinburgh from Glasgow or to come to Glasgow from Edinburgh
is the kettle through the boil? has the kettle boiled?

throughby OLDER SCOTS in the next room; into the next room

throwe't → NORTH EAST **to faa doon throwe't** to lapse unintentionally into the vernacular. This is said of someone who is attempting to speak posh and then gets it **wrang**.

thunder-plump thundery shower

tig → **to play tig** to play tag

tigh IN PLACE NAMES from the Gaelic ***taigh*** meaning *house*. So **Tighnabruaich**: house on the hill.

tilly IN PLACE NAMES from the Gaelic ***tullach*** meaning *hillock*. So **Tillicoultry**: (possibly) back land hill.

Tim SLANG derogatory for Catholic

tim empty

tim oot empty out

timeous LEGAL SCOTS In formal, official or legalistic Scots **timeous** means *done in or at the proper time.*

> **... which duties and obligations shall be executed in a diligent and timeous manner**

tink 1) rascal; mischievous child
2) NORTH EAST a dirty individual, a social outcast

tint OLDER SCOTS lost

tirrick SHETLAND arctic tern

tober IN PLACE NAMES from the Gaelic ***tobar*** meaning *well.* So **Tobermory**: Mary's well.

toffee NORTH EAST OLDER SCOTS In the North East **toffee** can be what elsewhere in Scotland is called **tablet**.

toon town

toonser NORTH EAST a townie; as opposed to a **teuchter**, who comes from the country

toorie SHETLAND knitted hat

tor IN PLACE NAMES from the Gaelic ***tòrr*** meaning *hill.* So **Kintore**: hill head.

torn-faced miserable looking

totty potato

toty wee tiny little

trachle NORTH EAST trudge; slog

trachled NORTH EAST harassed

Trades A traditional two-week industrial holiday in Aberdeen and Edinburgh, similar to the **Fair** in Glasgow.

trang SHETLAND busy; working well

trauchle NORTH EAST same as **trachle**

Treaty of Union This treaty, which came into force in May 1707, united Scotland and England under one parliament. They were to remain thus linked until 1999 when the Scottish parliament was re-established. Scotland's legal system and church have always remained independent.

trig 1) tidy; smart 2) alert

trip → **her face was tripping her** she was looking as miserable as sin, she had a face as long as a month of Sundays

tron In old Scottish towns goods and farm produce were weighed in a building called a **tron**, which housed the official public weighing scales. **The Trongate** is a major landmark in Glasgow.

trow SHETLAND similar to a *troll*

trucking barter

tube GLASGOW SLANG idiot

tumshie 1) turnip; swede 2) SLANG idiot

tushkar SHETLAND a spade used for cutting peat

twa OLDER SCOTS two

twal NORTH EAST twelve

twa-three NORTH EAST a couple (of), two or three

ty IN PLACE NAMES from the Gaelic ***taigh*** meaning *house*. So **Tyndrum**: house on the ridge.

tyne OLDER SCOTS lose

tystie SHETLAND black guillemot

U

uisge beatha [pronounced **oosh**gih **beh**-uh] whisky; literally in the Gaelic: water of life

unco OLDER SCOTS very

unco wheen OLDER SCOTS a great number

unnerstaun understand

Up-Helly-Aa Annual Viking fire festival in Shetland where the life-size replica of a Viking ship is set on fire and launched out to sea.

uplift

This has an additional meaning in Scots, with nothing of the spiritual about it at all: it simply means to *collect*.

we'll get a van round to uplift your old sofa next Tuesday

upset price another name, at an auction, for the reserve price

ur are

urnae aren't

V

voe SHETLAND bay, creek (an old Norse word)

W

waa NORTH EAST wall

wabbit knackered

wallies [pronounced to rhyme with SALLY'S] teeth

wally close tenement entrance and stairwell with tiled walls

wally dug (ornamental) china dog

wame NORTH EAST stomach, belly

wan [pronounced to rhyme with PAN] one

wance once

wark OLDER SCOTS work

warrant sale LEGAL SCOTS sale of some of a debtor's goods

wasted 1) drunk 2) exhausted 3) both of the former together

water → NORTH EAST **ower the water** in jail

watter → **doon the watter** down the Clyde on a pleasure steamer. Going **doon the watter** was a traditional Glasgow holiday; a boatload of families and couples and groups would sail down the Clyde to resorts such as Largs and Rothesay and the Kyles of Bute, traditionally (especially below decks) consuming vast quantities of alcohol.

wattrie NORTH EAST OLDER SCOTS toilet

wauner OLDER SCOTS wander

wayleave LEGAL SCOTS A right enabling land to be used by parties other than the owner, eg by the water authorities to lay pipes.

wean child; more of a Glaswegian and West of Scotland word; elsewhere the usual word is **bairn**

wecht NORTH EAST weight

wee little

Wee Free a member of the Free Church of Scotland; the term is, as it sounds, mocking and so obviously best not used to address such a church-goer directly. The Wee Frees are typically seen as the last bastion of good old traditional puritanism.

wee half a small whisky

wee heavy a very strong and sweetish beer, similar to barley wine

Weedjie Glaswegian, a term usually used by non-Glaswegians

weel SHETLAND NORTH EAST well

well

Can be moved to the end of a sentence in Scots, to lend emphasis.
put yer jaikit on well

well on nicely filled up with booze

well seen clear, obvious
it's well seen you've done that before it's obvious you've done that before

well-fired of a bread roll; very crisp, quite black on the outside

well-kent well-known

went → **I have went; he has went** etc
This is a common Scottish use of the preterite in place of the past participle. Some of those who use it in speech, would not use it in writing.

Western Isles another name for the Hebrides

wha, whae who

wheech move quickly

wheech away whip away

wheen → **a fair wheen of them** quite a number of them

wheesht same as **whisht**

whiles NORTH EAST sometimes

whin bush gorse bush

whin(s) gorse

whisht! quiet!, hush!, sh!
haud yer whisht be quiet, sh

whisky mac whisky with green ginger, amazing on a cold **dreich** day

whit what

white settler NORTH EAST If you've moved to the North East then you'll be a **white settler** not only if you come from England but if you come from any other part of Scotland too.

whitrat NORTH EAST OLDER SCOTS weasel

whulp puppy

whyles NORTH EAST sometimes

wi with

wide SLANG cheeky, out of order
they were pure getting wide they were pushing their luck

widna wouldn't

wide-o SLANG crook, conman, villain

> **this travel company's a bunch a wide-os, ah want ma money back!**

wifie NORTH EAST woman

> **the wifie that runs the sweetie shop**

wight OLDER SCOTS strong

wimplin winding

windae, windy window

that's wur pay rise oot ra windae that's our pay rise out the window

wir our

wis SHETLAND 1) was 2) us

wish → **do you wish another cup?** would you like another cup? This is not absurdly formal in Scots, as it would be in England.

workie workman

wrang wrong

writ LEGAL SCOTS legal document; not like an English writ, which is a summons

writer LEGAL SCOTS In legal Scots a writer is a lawyer. It's not a spoken form.

wur our

wursels ourselves

wye NORTH EAST way

wynd 1) lane 2) stone staircase, usually to the basement level of a house

wyte NORTH EAST know

Y

ya bass you bastard; also appended to names by grafitti-writing gangs, really just as an indication of attitude to the world

yacks SLANG eyes

> **there it was right under ma yacks**

yae NORTH EAST one

yaks same as **yacks**

yark NORTH EAST yank, jerk

ye you

yestreen OLDER SCOTS last night; yesterday evening

yett OLDER SCOTS gate

yin one (*people or things*)

> **have ye tried using a different yin?**
> **he's a strange yin, that Stanley**

yince once

yirded NORTH EAST filthy

yiz rendering of **youse**

yoal SHETLAND a type of six-oared boat

yon

> Means both the singular *that... (over there)* and the plural *those... (over*

there); unlike the antiquated word *yonder* in English, this is still in use in Scots, mainly in the east.

gies yon pair a pliers and haud the ladder still
what d'ye cry yon fella that's just become an MSP?

Yon can also be used to refer to a person.

he's nae match for big Shuggie, yon he's no match for big Shuggie, that guy over there

yon time late; a long time

it'll be yon time before we're hame

youse GLASGOW

This is a plural form of *you* – an area in which Scots comes closer in structure to other European languages; though it is a dialect form, not used by all, and those who do use it in speech wouldn't normally write it. It's useful to be able to distinguish though and make it clear that you are talking about a group not an individual.

youse played better today you all (you, the team) played better today

yowe ewe

Scottish Food and Drink

A Menu Reader

Scottish food and drink

Soups

broth thick, meal-in-a-plate type of soup, a staple item which varies according to the meat, fish, game or vegetables in season

cock-a-leekie traditional broth made with chicken, leeks, onions and rice

Cullen skink traditional broth (skink) of finnan haddock, potatoes, onion and milk from the fishing village of Cullen

ham and lentil broth traditional broth made with a ham bone, lentils, carrot, turnip and parsley

hotch potch traditional broth made with lamb and fresh seasonal vegetables

mussel broth traditional soup made with mussels in their shells, onions and cooking liquor

partan bree crab (partan) broth (bree) made with vegetables, thickened with rice and cream

Scotch broth traditional soup made with boiling beef, whole pearl barley and dried peas, fresh vegetables in season (usually including turnips and carrots) finished with chopped parsley

Main courses

Meat

Aberdeen Angus beef from cattle specially bred on Scotland's rich pasturelands for prime quality flavour and succulence

Arbroath smokie copper-coloured, deheaded, whole haddock, mildly salted, hot smoked till cooked, eaten heated with butter

blackface lamb hardy Scots breed of small-sized sheep with fine flavoured meat

bridie (Forfar) beef steak and onion filling in 'lucky' horseshoe-shaped short pastry crust (originally for bride's wedding meal)

brisket beef cut, often rolled and salted for boiling with root vegetables

buckie whelk

Forfar bridie *see* bridie

gigot leg of lamb

grouse medium sized game bird (one per portion) with a darker flesh and stronger flavour than most other game birds; usually roasted

guga (Solan goose) salted young gannet, traditional to the Hebrides, eaten with floury potato and a glass of milk

haggis supper chippie's version, sausage-shaped, coated in batter, deep fried and eaten with chips

haggis with neeps and tatties haggis made from sheep's innards, oatmeal, onion and spices, boiled in the stomach bag, traditionally eaten with mashed swedes/turnips (neeps) and mashed potatoes (tatties)

haunch of venison hind leg of deer meat from a red deer or a roe deer, usually roasted and served with rowan jelly

Highland beef from a special breed of hardy cattle with thick hairy coats, grazed on Scotland's rich pasturelands to yield high-quality succulent meat

hough (potted) [pronounced HOCH, with och as in LOCH] cut of beef from lower end of the leg or shin, cooked till tender and set in jelly

jugged hare slow-cooked mature hare stew, usually served with floury potato

Lorne sausage *see* square sausage

mealie pudding (white pudding) savoury sausage, with oatmeal and onions, often shaped in loops or as slicing sausage

mince and tatties minced beef, stewed with onions and sometimes carrots and turnips, served with mashed potatoes (tatties)

mutton mature, over a year old, sheep

pope's eye steak prime cut of beef from the rump end, grilled or fried, known in England as rump steak

reestit mutton *(Shetland)* cuts of mature sheep, salted, dried and used for flavouring broths, best cuts kept for Up-Helly-Aa festivities in January

rib eye steak prime cut of beef from the back with an 'eye' of fat in the middle for succulence

rumbledethumps mashed potatoes, cooked cabbage and butter mixed together and served in a pie dish with grated cheese on top

rump steak cut of beef from the rump end which is usually stewed in Scotland, it is a less tender cut than an English rump steak

sausage links beef or pork meat minced with seasonings and a starchy filler, used to fill sausage skins, divided into links

smokie (Arbroath) *see* Arbroath smokie

square sausage fresh beef sausage made in a square shaped tin, cut in slices and known in Glasgow as a Lorne sausage

stovies sliced potatoes, onions and dripping (surplus fat from cooking beef, lamb, pork or bacon) slow-cooked in a pot, sometimes with chopped meat added

white pudding *see* mealie pudding

Fish

Finnan haddock whole, split open haddock, lightly salted, delicately smoked, pale straw coloured, from the North East

fish 'n' chips deep-fried batter-coated fish (usually haddock) bought from the 'chippie' in Scotland, in the West eaten with salt and vinegar, in the East with salt and brown sauce

fried herring in oatmeal fresh filleted herring, pressed into oatmeal and shallow fried till brown on both sides, eaten with floury potatoes and butter

kipper (Mallaig kipper, Loch Fyne kipper) whole herring, split open, lightly salted and cold smoked, eaten at breakfast or teatime

potted herring filleted herring, rolled up and baked in vinegar and water with spices, served cold with salad

salt herring whole, gutted herring dry salted in barrels for several months, eaten with floury potatoes for 'tatties 'n' herrin'

soused herring same as potted herring

Vegetables

champit *or* **chappit tatties** mashed potatoes

clapshot *(Orkney)* mashed potatoes and turnips/swedes, beaten together and often served as vegetables with haggis

floury (or mealy) potato dry potato preferred in Scotland, popular varieties are Golden Wonder and Kerr's Pink

kail *or* **kale** traditional, hardy green winter vegetable of the cabbage family

neeps swedes, yellow turnips; traditional with haggis (neeps and tatties)

nettle green vegetable, tender young tops, eaten in springtime, often in a puréed soup

sybo spring onion

Side dishes

skirlie oatmeal, onions and dripping (surplus fat from cooking beef, lamb, pork or bacon) fried in a pan and eaten with floury potatoes or roast or stewed meat

Snacks

bacon and egg roll fried bacon and egg, served hot in a soft roll or bap for breakfast or snack

gammon roll soft roll filled with cooked ham, also known as gammon

Scotch pie small, hand-held, round, raised pie of cooked minced beef with top edge extending beyond the round of pastry covering the filling

tablet sweet confection made with butter, sugar and condensed milk, slightly harder in texture than fudge

Cheese

crowdie sharp, acidic, soft, cow's milk cheese either plain or with flavourings such as pepper and garlic

Dunlop cheese hard, pale yellow, cow's milk cheese from Ayrshire with a mellow, nutty flavour and creamy texture

Drinks

Atholl brose medium oatmeal soaked in whisky, sieved and flavoured with heather honey, taken at New Year

blended whisky mix of pot still malt whisky (40%) and patent still grain whisky (60%) from different distilleries

heather ale amber gold, flowery aromatic cask beer with a bitter note, made from heather flowers and sold by its Gaelic name 'Fraoch'

heavy beer; closest thing to English bitter

Irn Bru® orange-gold, carbonated, non-alcoholic drink with a sweet-spicy flavour and a citrus tang, often described as Scotland's other national drink

single and vatted malt whisky distilled in a pot still from fermenting malted barley, 'single' is the product of one distillery only, 'vatted' comes from a number of different malt whisky producing distilleries

whipkull whipped egg yolks, sugar and rum: a Shetland drink taken at New Year breakfast with shortbread

whisky mac whisky with green ginger wine: a warming drink in cold weather

Desserts

apple frushie open fruit tart, from an old Scots word for brittle or crumbly (referring to the pastry)

blaeberry like a bilberry

bramble black and juicy autumn berry, known in England as a blackberry

burnt cream rich cream custard with sugar crust 'burnt' on top to a hard crack

clootie dumpling large, celebration, spicy fruit pudding boiled in a cloth (clootie), served with custard or soft brown sugar (traditional for birthdays, Christmas and New Year); also sometimes fried with bacon and eggs for breakfast

crannachan harvest-home dish made by mixing cream and/or soft cream cheese with ripe soft berries, toasted oatmeal, heather honey and whisky

Ecclefechan butter tart open tart with a sweet buttery filling of dried fruit and walnuts

grosset fool gooseberry fool

Ingredients

Ayrshire bacon salt-cured pig, back and streaky cuts rolled into a round, cut thinly and cooked till crisp

heather honey thick, strongly aromatic, full-flavoured honey, gathered by bees from ling or bell heather

oatmeal made from the oat grain which is ground into fine, medium and coarse grades, Scotland's staple grain

rolled oats flaky oats, made by steaming and rolling whole oats, used for a quickly made porridge

whelk shellfish from Scotland's shores; the Scots whelk is an English winkle

Preserves

rowan jelly sweet preserve, made from whole rowan berries, served with venison and other game

Baking

Abernethy biscuit less rich shortbread made for his patients by the 18th century Dr Abernethy

bannock large round plain scone or rich yeast bread, originally baked on a large round iron girdle

bap soft white bread roll, dusted with flour, sometimes square-shaped

beremeal bannock *(Orkney)* [pronounced BARE-meal] flat, round, girdle baked, teatime bread made with ancient bere (barley) grown in Orkney and the North

black bun dense cake with dried fruits, highly spiced and enclosed in a pastry crust: a New Year speciality with whisky

buttery rowie *(Aberdeen)* misshapen, flaky, crisp roll (rowie), original to the North East, a croissant without the elegant shape

cookie rich yeast bun, eaten at teatime

cream cookie rich teatime yeasted bun, sliced open, filled with whipped cream and dusted on top with icing sugar

crumpet thinner and larger than the Scots pancake, girdle-baked, smooth on one side and lacy on the other, eaten rolled up with butter and/or jam for afternoon tea

currant loaf light, sweet, yeasted bread, traditionally eaten at teatime, sometimes toasted with butter

dropped scones alternative name for Scotch pancakes, 'dropped' onto the girdle

Dundee cake fruit cake with sultanas, orange peel and whole almonds on top, originally a by-product of marmalade making in Dundee

gingerbread spicy fruit loaf made with treacle and ginger, eaten at teatime

girdle scone any kind of sweet or savoury scone baked on a heated flat iron plate, known as a girdle

oatcake thin, crisp, savoury biscuit made with oatmeal: originally baked on the girdle and eaten with butter and cheese as a staple item of diet

pancake (Scotch) sweet, golden brown, flat round disc, made with the same batter mixture as Scotch crumpet: eaten with butter and jam at teatime (an American pancake is its larger version); not like crêpe

petticoat tails shortbread round, cut in wedges but with a small circle cut out of the centre, resembling the crinoline petticoat

potato scone same as tattie scone

rowie crisp roll (also called **Aberdeenshire buttery**)

Selkirk bannock rich, buttery, round, curved on top, yeasted bread with sultanas: sliced and toasted with butter for tea

shortbread butter, sugar and flour, blended and shaped into rounds, fingers or triangles, baked slowly till pale golden and crisp

soda scone round plain scone, baked on a girdle, eaten with butter and jam for tea

softie round, yeasted, slightly sweet, soft morning roll from the North East, (as distinct from the harder buttery rowie)

square loaf straight-sided loaf with close-textured soft crumb sides, slices cut in half used to sandwich the Lorne/square sausage

tattie scone thin, unleavened triangular-shaped scone, made with a mixture of mashed potatoes and flour, baked on both sides till brown on a girdle

sundries

black pudding blood sausage, flavoured with spices, oatmeal and onion, usually shaped in loops or as slicing sausage; accompanies a traditional breakfast

brose dish made from oatmeal and water or milk

porridge fine, medium or coarse oatmeal boiled in water till thick, seasoned with salt and eaten for breakfast with milk or cream

Here's a smattering of Gaelic.

good morning
madainn mhath
[madeen **va**]

hello (*during the day*)
latha math
[laa **ma**]

good evening
feasgar math
[fesgar **ma**]

good night
oidhche mhath
[uh-ee-*kh*ih **va**]

goodbye
slàn leibh
[**slaan** luh-eev]

thanks
tapadh leibh
[tah-puh **luh-eev**]

thank you very much
òran taing
[moh-ran **ta-eenk**]

not for me
chan ann dhomhsa
[*kh*an a-oon gh**oh**suh]

please
mas e ur toil e
[mash uh oor **tol** uh]

Buy a Gael a dram and ask him/her to tell you how to say 'l' here!

the *kh* as in Ba*ch*, lo*ch*

Buy a Gael a dram and ask him/her to tell you how to say 'gh'!

great!
math dha-rìribh!
[ma gha **ree**riv]

good
math
[ma]

that one
am fear sin
[ihm **fair** shin]

this one
am fear seo
[ihm **fair** sho]

not that one
chan e am fear sin
[*kh*any**eh** ihm fair shin]

I like it
's toil leam e
[**stul** luhmuh]

I don't like it
cha toil leam e
[*kh*a **tul** luhmuh]

cheers!
slàinte! *or* slàinte mhòr!
[sl**aa**ntjuh, slaantjuh **vor**]

that was excellent
bha sin sgoinneil
[va shin **skun**yel]

I don't understand
chan eil mi a' tuigsinn
[*kh*an yel mee uh **teek**shin]

There are no words given here for *yes* or *no*, because Gaelic is one of those languages that doesn't have a single way of saying *yes* or *no*. It all depends on what the question or statement is to which yes/no is the response.

... with strange-sounding names

Here are some Scottish names which are not pronounced as you might think.

Alford	AA-ford
Ballachulish	BallaHOOlish
Berwick	Berrick
Broughty Ferry	Brotty Ferry
Buccleuch	Buh-KLOO
Buchanan	Byou-KANan
Cockburn	COH-burn
Colintravie	Colin-TRYVE
Colquhoun	Co-HOON
Crichton	CRY-ton
Culross	CURE-oss
Culzean	Cuh-LAYN
Dalry	Dal-RYE
Dalziel	Dee-EL
Fionnphort	Finnerfort
Glamis	Glams
Hawick	Hoyk
Ingliston	Ingleston
Islay	Isle-uh
Kingussie	Kin-YOU-see
Kirkcaldy	KirCODdee
Kirkcudbright	KirCUDbree
Leuchars	LOO-kers
Milngavie	Mul-GUY
Moray	Murray
Sanquhar	Sanker
Scone	Skoon
Strathaven	STRAYven
Urquhart	URkurt
Wemyss Bay	Weems Bay

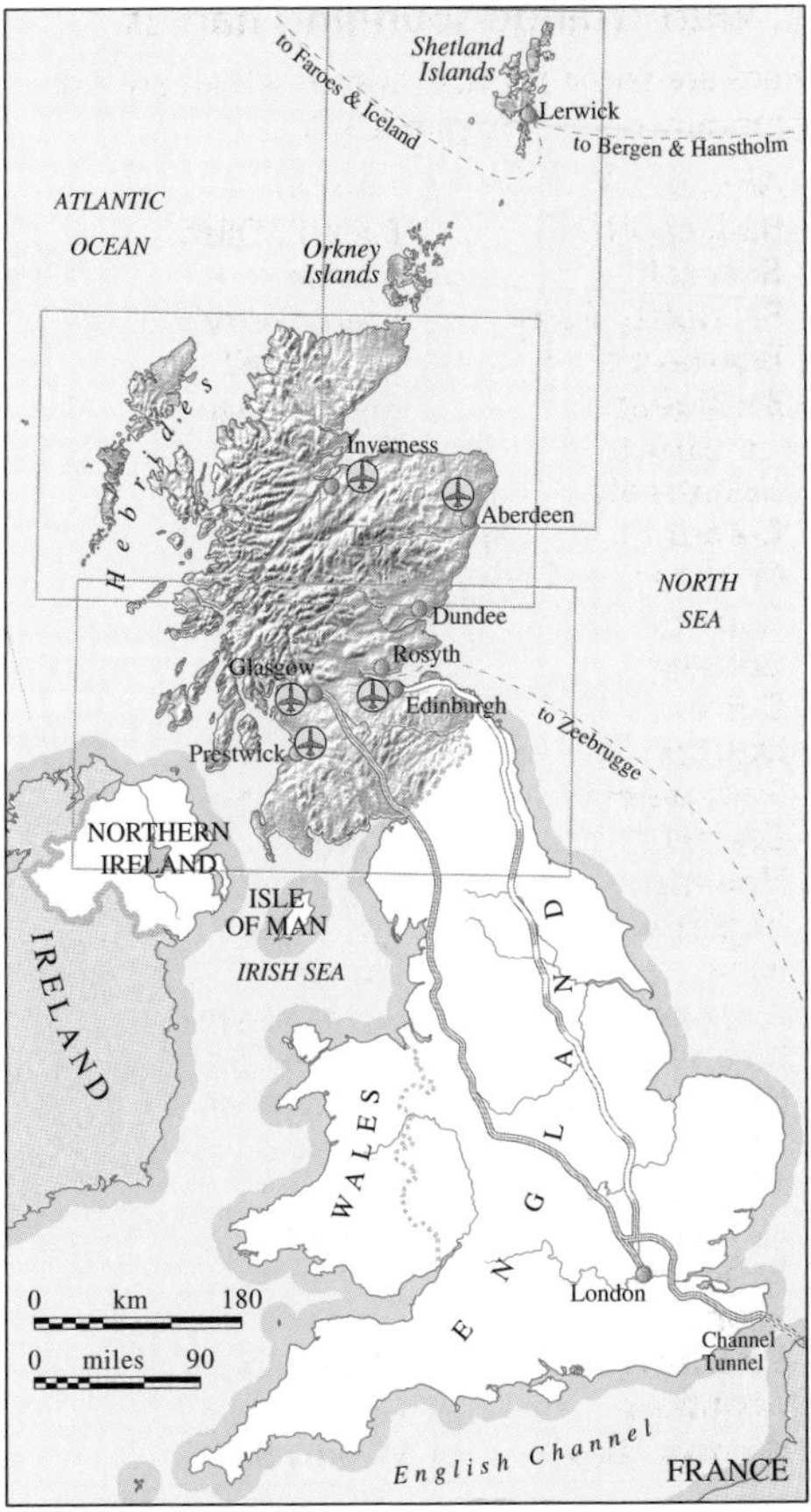
to Faroes & Iceland
Shetland Islands
Lerwick
to Bergen & Hanstholm
ATLANTIC OCEAN
Orkney Islands
Hebrides
Inverness
Aberdeen
NORTH SEA
Dundee
Rosyth
Glasgow
Edinburgh
to Zeebrugge
Prestwick
NORTHERN IRELAND
ISLE OF MAN
IRISH SEA
IRELAND
WALES
ENGLAND
London
Channel Tunnel
0 km 180
0 miles 90
English Channel
FRANCE

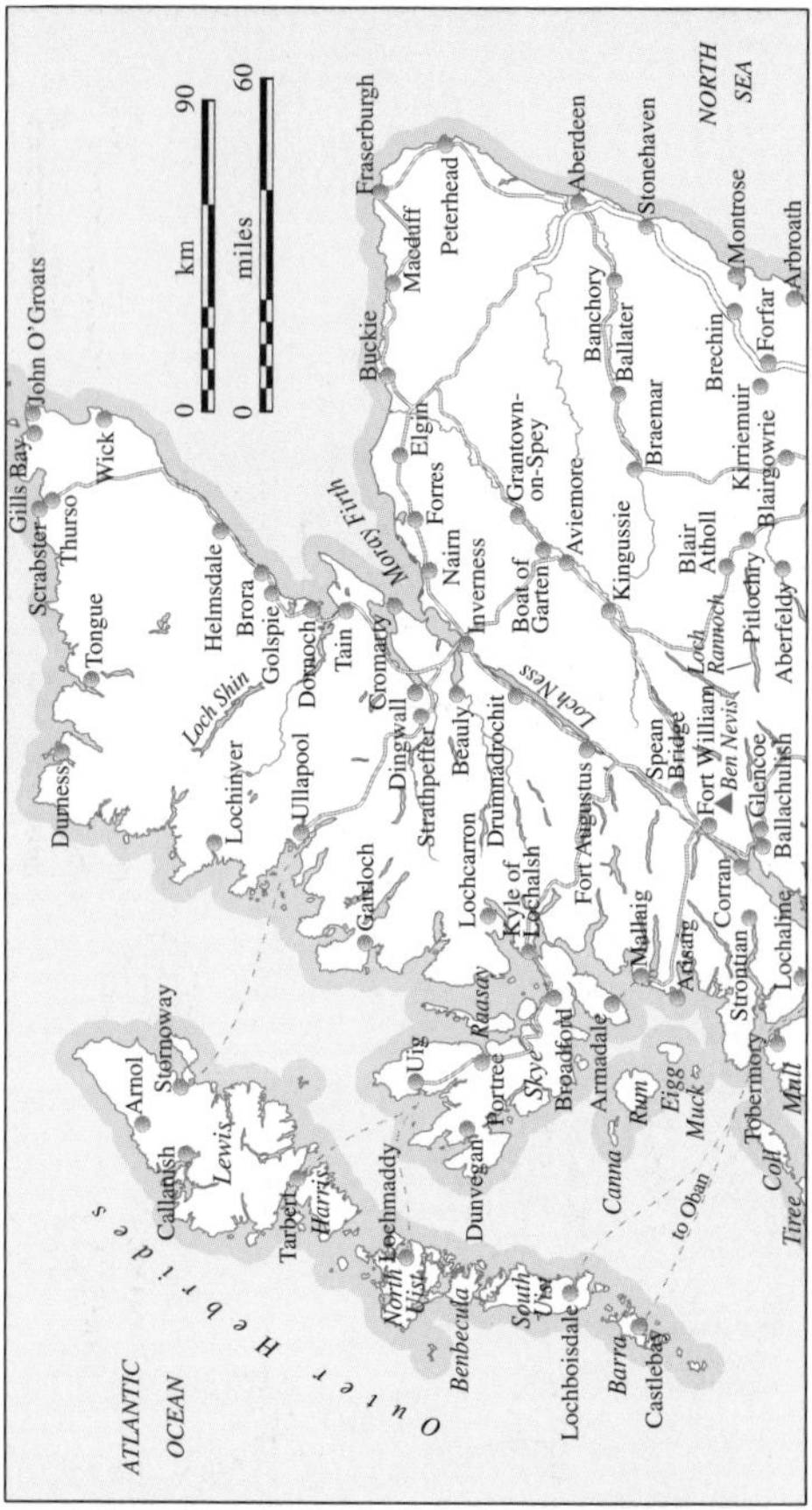
ATLANTIC
OCEAN
Outer Hebrides
NORTH
SEA
0 km 90
0 miles 60
John O'Groats
Gills Bay
Wick
Thurso
Scrabster
Tongue
Durness
Helmsdale
Brora
Golspie
Loch Shin
Lochinver
Ullapool
Dornoch
Tain
Cromarty
Dingwall
Strathpeffer
Beauly
Drumnadrochit
Lochcarron
Kyle of Lochalsh
Gairloch
Fort Augustus
Loch Ness
Inverness
Nairn
Forres
Elgin
Buckie
Moray Firth
Fraserburgh
Macduff
Peterhead
Aberdeen
Stonehaven
Montrose
Arbroath
Banchory
Ballater
Braemar
Brechin
Forfar
Kirriemuir
Blairgowrie
Grantown-on-Spey
Aviemore
Kingussie
Boat of Garten
Blair Atholl
Pitlochry
Aberfeldy
Loch Rannoch
Spean Bridge
Fort William
Ben Nevis
Glencoe
Ballachulish
Corran
Ardgour
Mallaig
Lochaline
Strontian
Tobermory
Mull
Coll
Tiree
Arnol
Stornoway
Callanish
Lewis
Tarbert
Harris
Lochmaddy
North Uist
Benbecula
South Uist
Lochboisdale
Barra
Castlebay
Uig
Portree
Raasay
Skye
Dunvegan
Broadford
Armadale
Canna
Rum
Eigg
Muck
to Oban

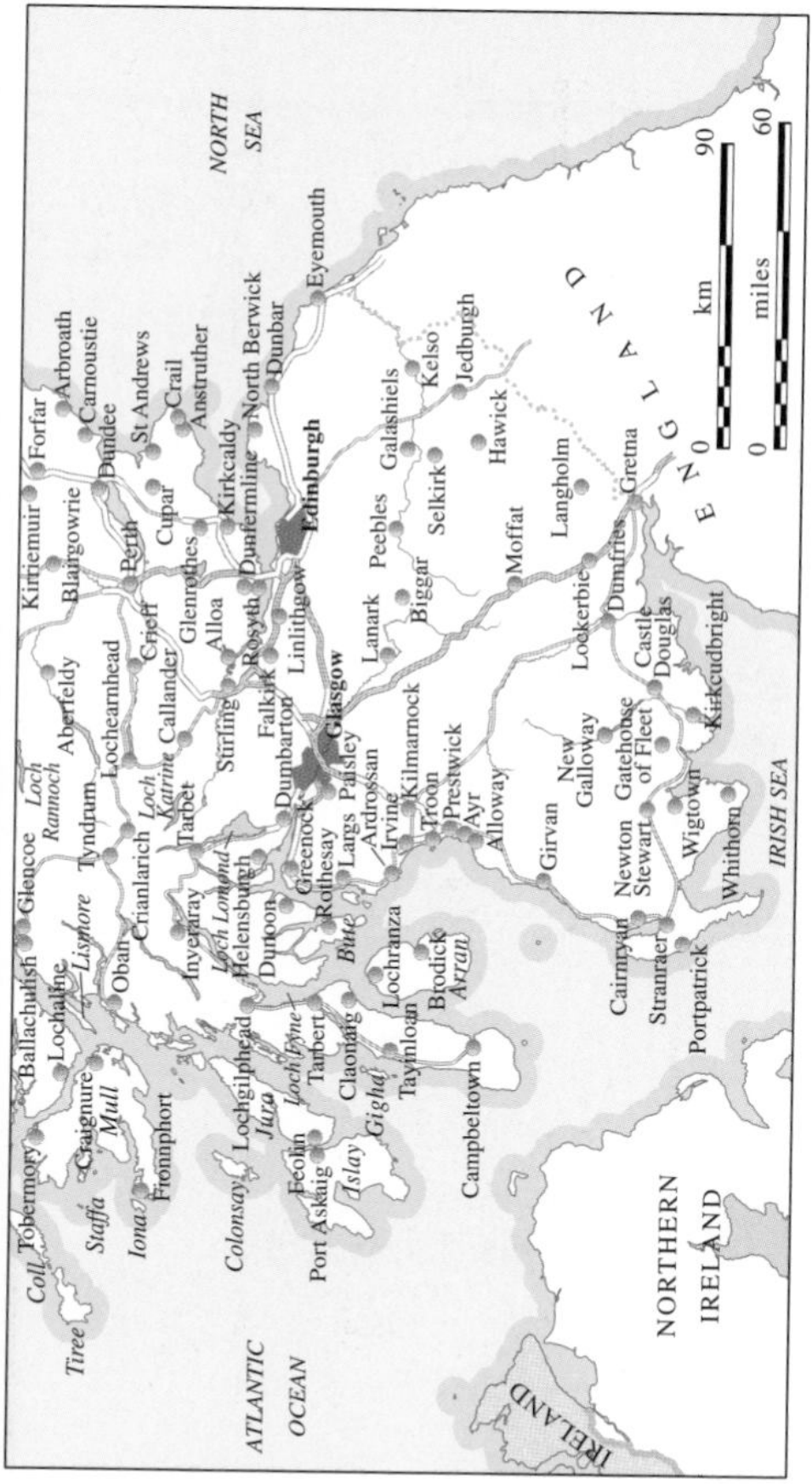
NORTH SEA
ENGLAND
0 km 90
0 miles 60
Eyemouth
North Berwick
Dunbar
Arbroath
Carnoustie
Forfar
St Andrews
Crail
Anstruther
Dundee
Kirkcaldy
Dunfermline
Edinburgh
Kirriemuir
Blairgowrie
Perth
Cupar
Glenrothes
Alloa
Crieff
Rosyth
Linlithgow
Aberfeldy
Callander
Falkirk
Stirling
Lochearnhead
Glasgow
Dumbarton
Paisley
Ardrossan
Kilmarnock
Irvine
Troon
Prestwick
Ayr
Alloway
Girvan
Kelso
Jedburgh
Galashiels
Hawick
Selkirk
Peebles
Biggar
Lanark
Moffat
Langholm
Gretna
Dumfries
Lockerbie
Castle Douglas
Kirkcudbright
New Galloway
Gatehouse of Fleet
Newton Stewart
Wigtown
Whithorn
Cairnryan
Stranraer
Portpatrick
Glencoe
Loch Rannoch
Tyndrum
Loch Katrine
Tarbet
Inveraray
Loch Lomond
Helensburgh
Dunoon
Greenock
Rothesay
Largs
Butte
Lochranza
Brodick
Arran
Campbeltown
Tayinloan
Claonaig
Tarbert
Loch Fyne
Gigha
Islay
Beoiln
Port Askaig
Lochgilphead
Jura
Colonsay
Oban
Crianlarich
Lisphore
Lochaline
Ballachulish
Craignure
Mull
Fionnphort
Iona
Staffa
Tobermory
Coll
Tiree
ATLANTIC OCEAN
IRISH SEA
NORTHERN IRELAND
IRELAND

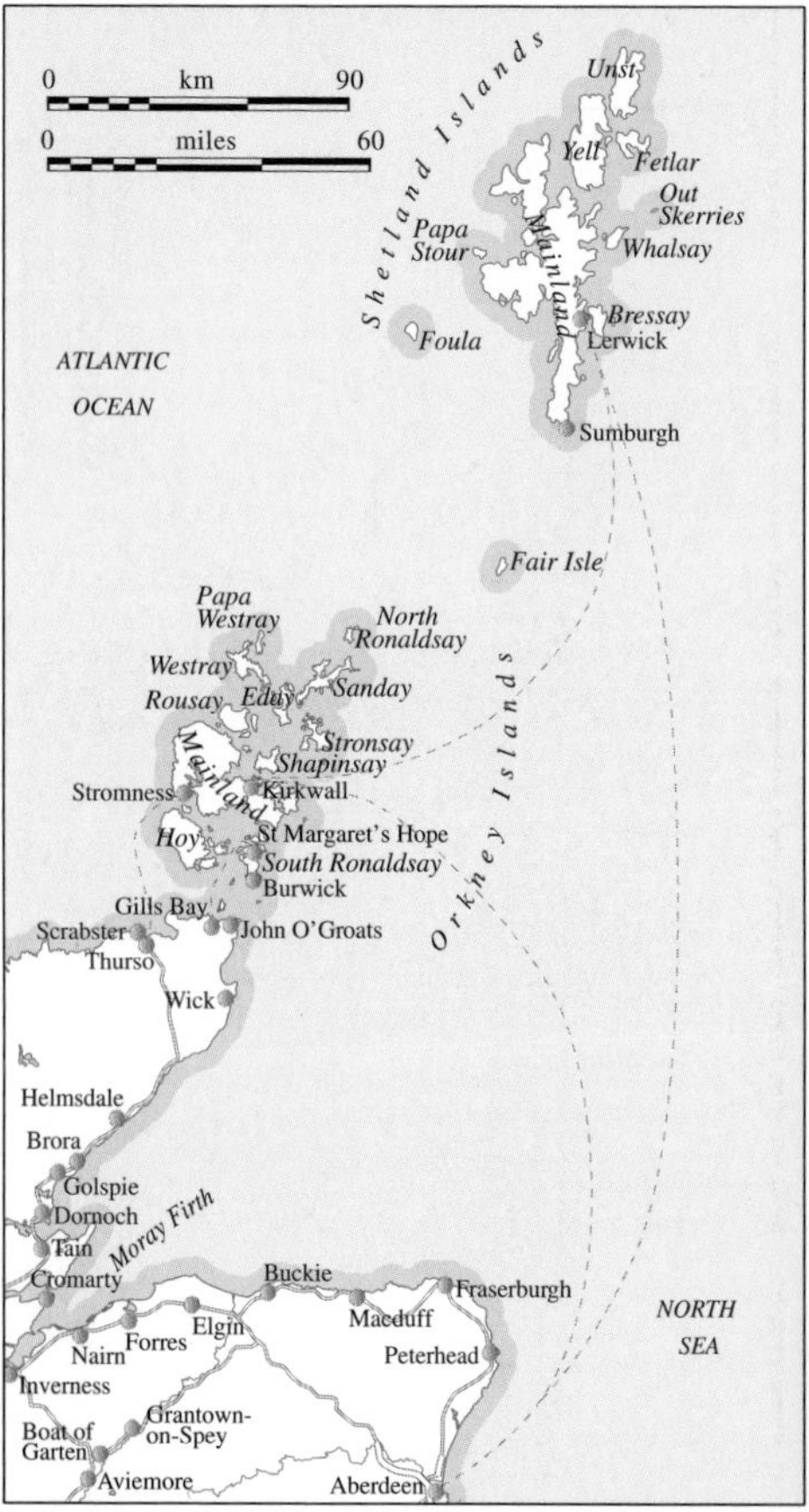
0 km 90
0 miles 60
Shetland Islands
Unst
Yell
Fetlar
Out Skerries
Whalsay
Papa Stour
Mainland
Bressay
Lerwick
Foula
ATLANTIC OCEAN
Sumburgh
Fair Isle
Papa Westray
North Ronaldsay
Westray
Sanday
Rousay
Eday
Stronsay
Shapinsay
Mainland
Kirkwall
Stromness
Hoy
St Margaret's Hope
South Ronaldsay
Burwick
Orkney Islands
Gills Bay
Scrabster
John O'Groats
Thurso
Wick
Helmsdale
Brora
Golspie
Dornoch
Tain
Moray Firth
Cromarty
Buckie
Fraserburgh
Elgin
Macduff
Forres
Nairn
Peterhead
NORTH SEA
Inverness
Grantown-on-Spey
Boat of Garten
Aviemore
Aberdeen